BASIC ILLUSTRATED

Poisonous and Psychoactive Plants

BASIC ILLUSTRATED

Poisonous and Psychoactive Plants

Jim Meuninck

GUILFORD, CONNECTICUT
HELENA, MONTANA

Copyright © 2014 Rowman & Littlefield

FalconGuides is an imprint of Globe Pequot Press.
Falcon, FalconGuides, and Outfit Your Mind are registered trademarks of Rowman & Littlefield.

All photos by Jim Meuninck unless otherwise noted.

Project editor: Lauren Szalkiewicz
Layout: Mary Ballachino

Library of Congress Cataloging-in-Publication data is available on file.

ISBN 978-0-7627-9190-3

Distributed by NATIONAL BOOK NETWORK

Contents

Acknowledgments

This book represents the efforts of many individuals. I would like to acknowledge the expertise and professionalism of copy editor Kathy Brock. Thank you, Kathy. And thank you Melissa Evarts for the creative layout and design of the book. I would also like to thank the entire GPP staff and especially acquisitions editor David Legere whose hard work and dedication made this journey most rewarding. Behind the scenes JC found the elusive buckeye, Joseph led me to San Pedro and Peyote, and daughter Becca went to Brazil and returned with one fabulous coffee bean photo. Spouse Jill stood by assisting, consoling, and accepting my physical presence and mental absence. It is finished. And I am back. Let's have fun!

Introduction

Pity the poor plants, firmly rooted, ensconced between rocks, stuck without arms and legs, unable to run and hide or defend themselves. They appear vulnerable, easy prey—food for man and beast, for insects, viruses, fungi, and bacteria. Yet, given all these handicaps they persist and flourish, paving the earth in color, sheltering the wilderness in timber and flowering our plates with sensual perfume and mouth-watering flavors. How is this possible? What makes them so successful? Chemistry! Yes, chemistry! Plants are prolific chemical factories producing prodigious amounts of unique compounds that stagger the mind, that resist the burning sun, that poison and incapacitate, that burn and itch, that empty the bowels and flush the stomach.Their chemical stew chokes lungs, swells sinuses, starts the heart, and purges the brain. See them there, sessile and brave, nakedly defying the elements, hiding under the sheltering tree, distilling poison—they are the alpha and omega, the food for all life, without them nothing exists. Make no mistake: Plants are the best thing to happen to you and this planet, so revel in their presence. Know their potential or pay the price of ignorance.

Your quest for knowledge begins here, in the wild places of our planet uncovering the secrets of the unheralded gatekeepers of life. Start by reading chapter introductions to get a feel for content. Page through the book and see what plants you instantly recognize. Pause and explore the ones that intrigue. Take this guide into the field and into the garden. Paw it dirty. Stash it next to the commode within easy reach. Enjoy every page, again and again, until the book, the plants, and you are one. Then go forth, my friend, arrogantly, secure in the knowledge that all plants, the good, the bad and the ugly, have a purpose, and that purpose is you.

Poisonous Wild Plants

Wild plants with toxic properties pose potential threats to you, your children, livestock, and pets. If you cannot identify a plant, call your local extension center or home and garden education center for assistance. It is also important to realize many toxic plants must be consumed in considerable quantities for poisoning to occur, and often poisonous plants taste bitter or acrid, keeping children and pets from ingesting large amounts. Teach young children not to put unknown plants or plant parts in their mouths.

If a child or anyone ingests a potentially poisonous plant, call your family doctor or nearest emergency room immediately. The number for the American Association of Poison Control Centers is (800) 222-1222. They can tell you if a plant is poisonous and what symptoms to expect with a particular toxin. Be prepared to provide the identity of the plant, time ingested, and presenting symptoms.

Chapter One

Poisonous Wild Plants

In our wild places, toxic plants grow side by side with edible wild plants. Therefore, it is necessary for the intrepid forager to know the difference. Mistakenly eating poisonous lookalikes account for many of the calls to hospital emergency rooms. To avoid this life-threatening inconvenience, learn what to look for and what to avoid. Here are a number of poisonous plants that grow in fields, forests, and wet areas. Find them, know them, and avoid them. Avoid their chemistry and live a long life.

AMERICAN LIVERWORT

Ranunculaceae *(Hepatica americana)*

Sharp leaved hepatica. (Hepatica acutiloba)

Identification: Low-lying plant with liver-shaped leaves is one of the first flowers of spring. Six to eight petal flowers vary from white to blue. Compound leaves have 3 lobes. Stems and petioles are fragile and covered with silky white hairs. Plant grows to 6" in height in small colonies.

Habitat: Typically found in hardwood forests around or near the base of trees—east of the Prairie to the East Coast, north to Ontario, and south to the Gulf.

Toxins: Fresh plant is toxic in high doses. Toxin is ranunculin and its derivatives. Drying or cooking the plant denatures toxic chemistry.

Symptoms: Extended skin contact with fresh plant and plant juices may cause dermatitis and produce difficult-to-heal blisters. Internally, protoanemonin is caustic to mucous membranes and may irritate the intestinal tract and urinary tract. Diarrhea and colic are symptomatic.

First Aid: First aid for external contact and blistering is gentle cool-water irrigation; in professional medical treatment the physician may irrigate with dilute anti-infective potassium permanganate and then apply emollients. Ingestion may require gastric lavage and administration of activated charcoal, plus rehydration.

ARROW ARUM

Araceae *(Peltandra virginica)*

Identification: Arrow-shaped leaf, pinnate veins; green primitive-looking flower producing numerous pea-size seeds; often grows in large colonies in and around spatterdock (yellow pond lilies).

Habitat: Wetland plant, edges of streams, marshes, fens. Grows in water and found across the United States except in desert areas and subtropical biomes.

Toxins: All parts of the plant, including the flower and mature fruit, contain toxic calcium oxalate crystals.

Symptoms: Eating the fresh plant feels as if sharp needles are hammered into your tongue, and the pain continues through the digestive system if swallowed. This burning sensation can induce copious sweating and panic, including airway obstruction. Contact with fresh juice may produce painful blistering.

First Aid: If swallowed, call a physician. Skin treatment requires copious water irrigation, although the irritant is more soluble in vinegar. For oral exposures, physically remove any plant material from the mouth. Check for compromised airway; if it is not, consume cold liquids, ice cream, Popsicles, or crushed ice for relief. A physician may administer diphenhydramine elixir, providing anesthetic and antihistaminic effects. A compromised-airway treatment requires antihistamines, hospital admission, and observation until the edema improves.

Eye exposures are treated with copious water irrigation. A physician may employ slit-lamp examination and fluorescein staining to rule out corneal involvement.

Note: Avoid problems by cooking any arums or arum parts you eat above 200°F, which degrades the toxin. This acute irritant (calcium oxalate) was used to punish slaves.

BANEBERRY, RED AND WHITE; BUGBANE
Ranunculaceae (*Actaea rubra, A. pachypoda*)

Identification: Born on a creeping rootstock and sending up erect, triangular stems, these perennials grow 1'–2' high, sparingly branched, and presenting footstalks that divide into 3 smaller footstalks; redivided so that each leaf is composed of 18–27 dark-green hairless or slightly downy leaflets. The June flower stem arises solitary from the root and

White baneberry

has leaves of the same form, but smaller. Flowers are pure white, maturing into egg-shaped, many-seeded red or white berries, depending on the species.

Habitat: Found in the North Temperate Zone from the East Coast to the West Coast and south to New Mexico and north into Canada. Typically in forested areas; shade tolerant.

Toxins: Ranunculin in baneberry releases the toxic chemical protoanemonin enzymatically whenever the plant is damaged, such as by chewing, hand picking, or pulping.

Symptoms: Protoanemonin is a skin irritant, causing redness and blistering of the skin. It has a similar effect on the mucous membranes of the esophagus, stomach, and intestines when ingested. The first symptoms of baneberry poisoning are burning and blistering in the mouth and throat, followed by nausea, intestinal cramps, diarrhea, and renal damage. Conjectured doses of the cardiogenic toxins in 6 or more berries may induce respiratory distress, ventricular fibrillation, and—theoretically—cardiac arrest. Although there are no reports of adult fatalities, there are historical references to deaths of children.

First Aid: For significant ingestion, gastric lavage is administered (saline solution entered into and then siphoned from the stomach), followed by the consumption of a demulcent such as egg whites in milk. Keep victim hydrated. Skin irritation responds favorably to copious irrigation with cool water.

Note: The berries are quite bitter, so it is unlikely that an individual would continue to eat them after tasting one—bitterness (the taste of alkaloids) is the taste of toxicity.

BITTERSWEET NIGHTSHADE AND BLACK NIGHTSHADE
Solanaceae (*Solanum nigrum, S. dulcamara, S. americanum*)

Solanum dulcamara

Identification: This is a very large genus with over 1,700 species. Bittersweet nightshade is a climbing vine found clinging to shrubs in wetlands, with purple rocket-shaped flowers and bearing a reddish-orange fruit. Leaves are lobed and alternate. Black nightshade (*S. nigrum*) is an erect, spreading plant growing to 5' (but typically smaller) with alternate leaves, thornless stems, with white to light purple flowers with yellow centers giving way to clusters of black berries.

Habitat: Along wetlands, shores, stream banks, in fields and waste ground across the eastern states and as far west as the state of Washington. Black nightshade prefers drier soil and sometimes overlaps in horse nettle.

Toxins: Solanin, glycoalkaloids, and solasodine—the latter typically in higher concentrations in unripe berries of black nightshade, making the unripe berries particularly dangerous.

Symptoms: Consumption is rarely fatal in adults but more toxic in children—several hours after consumption a scratchy, irritated throat manifests, perhaps with fever and diarrhea. Symptoms may persist. See a physician. Keep victim hydrated.

First Aid: Treat as a medical emergency, evacuate, or seek professional medical help.

Note: Eating the unripe, green berries of black nightshade has taken the lives of children. Teach your children well! Bittersweet nightshade is a traditional external remedy for skin abrasions and inflammation. Stems have been approved by the German Commission E (the commissioned scientific advisory board for herbal and folk medicine) for external use as therapy in chronic eczema.

BLUEFLAG, WILD IRIS
Iridaceae (*Iris versicolor*)

Identification: Swordlike leaves 2'–3' long; blue to violet, irregular-shaped flower, orchid like. Plant springs from a shallow rhizome. The bladed leaves typically have a gray-blue tint and are flat.

Habitat: Wetland plant found in damp marshes, fens, bogs, and along streams and the edges of lakes. It transplants to the garden and is resplendent.

Iris versicolor

Toxins: Iridin and irisin are toxic, acrid resinous irritants (found in rootstocks of numerous species in this genus).

Symptoms: May induce nausea and vomiting.

First Aid: Rehydration (fluid replacement). In acute cases evacuate to medical help.

Note: There is an unrelated irisin compound studied in weight-loss therapy. Prior to blooming, wild iris can be confused with edible cattail shoots. Remember that cattail stems do not have the gray-blue tint and are round or oval shaped instead of flat.

BUCKEYE, HORSE CHESTNUT

Hippocastanaceae (*Aesculus hippocastanum*)

Identification: Medium-size tree. Compound leaves are composed of 5 fine-toothed leaflets. Fruit has thick, knobby, spined husk covering a shiny brown seed. Dried leaves and nut oil used as medicine.

Habitat: Fields and edges of woods in Temperate Zone from coast to coast, from California, Ontario, and Quebec across the straits into Newfoundland.

Toxins: Active compounds are triterpene saponins, rutin, quercitrin, and isoquercitrin. Cytotoxic chemicals are a cluster of saponins called aescins.

Symptoms: Ingestion of nut or end twigs leads to severe gastroenteritis.

First Aid: Hydrate with tepid water, administer electrolytes (Gatorade will work) and demulcents such as Kaeopectate, Mylanta, or milk of magnesia.

BUCKTHORN, CASCARA SAGRADA

Rhamnaceae (*Rhamnus cathartica, Rhamnus purshiana*)

Identification: Small shrubs or trees, from 4'–20' tall, many branched, and densely foliated. When mature, bark is gray-brown with gray-white lenticels (spots). Leaves are thin, bladelike, and hairy on the ribs, fully margined, elliptical to ovate, and 2" in length. Greenish-white flowers are numerous and grow on axillary cymes. Small white flowers with 5 petals grow in clusters. Ripe fruit is red to purple-black with 2 or 3 seeds. *R. purshiana* is taller, to 30', with leaves that have 20–24 veins.

Rhamnus purshiana

Habitat: *R. purshiana* grows in the foothills of British Columbia, Idaho, Washington, Montana, and Oregon. Another small shrub-like *R. cathartica* grows throughout the dunelands of Lake Michigan.

Toxins: Contains highly cathartic anthraquinones, hydroxyanthracene, and emodin from the fruit and bark.

Symptoms: Nausea, vomiting, and catharsis.

Rhamnus *sp., Lake Michigan Dunes*

First Aid: Have a toilet handy. Condition is self-limiting; rehydrate.

Note: Pharmaceutical preparations to speed bowel function should not be used by pregnant women.

CASTOR BEAN, AFRICAN COFFEE TREE, CASTOR OIL PLANT
Euphorbiaceae (*Ricinus communis*)

Identification: Annual plant, 15'–40' tall; leaves with 5–12 large cleft lobes; glossy and coarsely toothed leaves up to 1' across, typically dark green when mature (perhaps with a reddish tinge, variable). Stems and the spherical, spiny seed capsules also vary in pigmentation. Both male and female flowers are borne on a spike: Male flowers are yellowish green with creamy white stamens; female flowers are borne on tips of spikes with prominent red stigmas. Fruit is a spiny, greenish (to reddish-purple) capsule containing large, oval, shiny, bean-like, highly poisonous seeds with brownish mottling. Castor seeds have an insect-attracting appendage called a caruncle that insures the dispersion of the seed.

Habitat: West Indies, Mexico, and broadly distributed in the United States in the wild and as an ornamental cultivar.

Toxins: Ricin is a potent biological toxin and can be lethal in children and adults after eating as few as 4–8 seeds.

Symptoms: Actual poisoning is rare, attributed to the rather painful and unpleasant symptoms of overdosing on ricin, which can include nausea, diarrhea, tachycardia, hypotension, and seizures persisting for up to a week. These symptoms may be delayed up to 36 hours but commonly begin within 2–4 hours and include pain and burning in mouth and throat, abdominal pain, vomiting, and bloody diarrhea, after which there is severe dehydration, a drop in blood pressure, and decreased urination, culminating in death.

First Aid: Treatment is entirely in a hospital setting, requiring gastric lavage and the use of activated charcoal to bind the ricin, with ongoing fluid and electrolyte replacement. Hospitalization may be necessary for up to 2 weeks.

Note: *Guinness Book of Records* claimed the castor bean plant as the most poisonous plant in the world; however, fatalities and suicides are rare due to the foulness of the drug and perverse symptoms of intoxication. Ricin was used as a terrorist weapon, sent in envelopes through the mail to politicians and other officials.

CREOSOTE BUSH

Zygophylaceae (*Larrea tridentata*)

Identification: Resinous and aromatic shrub 3'–10' tall with reddish-brown bark near the base with lighter to almost white bark higher up and on limbs and branches. Small, yellow-green leaves have a glossy, leathery look and texture. Tiny flowers are yellow and develop into fuzzy (hairy) seed-bearing capsules.

Habitat: Desert inhabitant of the southwestern United States and Mexico.

Toxins: The commercial and medical use of chaparral is suspect due to concern over its potential toxic effect upon the liver, causing subacute or acute hepatitis. Lignan chemistry of chaparral is well studied, and extensive literature has been published on the principal component, nordihydroguaiaretic acid (NDGA), which is a powerful antioxidant that in animal studies has been shown to have both anticancerous and cancerous effects. Because of the cancer-causing potential, the questions concerning liver toxicity, and the unproven uses of the herb, consider an alternative to chaparral. On December 21, 2005, Health Canada warned consumers not to ingest the herb chaparral in the form of loose leaves, teas, capsules, or bulk herbal products because of the risk of liver and kidney problems. In the United States, commercial sale of the herb is banned. Holistic health-care professionals may still recommend and use the herb, but it is this author's contention that chaparral be avoided until evidence of efficacy and safety are scientifically established.

Symptoms: Carcinogenic; liver failure.

First Aid: Avoidance.

Note: One reason for chaparral's great success is the presence of a highly toxic substance produced in and released from its root that prevents other plants from growing nearby. Rainfall washes away the toxin, allowing other plants to grow. Once the water drains off, the toxin is released again, and the invading plants are destroyed. This ability ensures that chaparral does not have to compete with other plant life for scarce nutrients.

A decoction of the evergreen leaves of the creosote bush has been used by various North American Indian tribes to treat diarrhea and stomach problems. Documented uses: A poultice of the chewed plant was placed over insect, spider, and snakebites. Wash of leaf infusion has been used to increase milk flow. Sap from heated twigs was packed into cavities to treat toothache; a leaf poultice was applied to wounds, skin problems, and as a therapy for chest complaints. Native American uses included it as a treatment for rheumatic disease, venereal infections, urinary infections, and cancer, especially leukemia. A tea made from the leaves may be taken internally as an expectorant and pulmonary antiseptic. It has been used to treat many conditions, including fever, influenza, colds, gas, arthritis, sinusitis, anemia, fungal infections, allergies, autoimmune diseases, and premenstrual syndrome (PMS); it is also considered an analgesic, antidiarrhetic, diuretic, and emetic.

DATURA, JIMSONWEED
Solanaceae (*Datura stramonium, D. meteloides*)

Identification: The hollow stem is upright or branched and grows 3'– 4' high. Trumpetlike white to light violet flower is distinctive. Seed capsules are studded with spines. Leaves are long stemmed, toothed, and coarse textured. Crushed leaves and stems have a pungent odor.

Habitat: Found along roadsides, disturbed ground, and in bean and corn fields throughout the United States,

D. meteloides is more common in the Southwest and Four Corners area. It is a popular, showy garden flower throughout the Midwest. The plant, with all its spines, fairly screams, "Stay away!"

Toxins: Belladonna alkaloids, which include scopolamine, atropine, and hyoscyamine (also called daturine).

Symptoms: Dry mouth, intoxication, dilated pupils, perhaps reddening of face and neck, delirium, hallucinations, tachycardia, and elevated blood pressure—severe overdose with as few as 20 seeds may lead to death.

First Aid: Severe intoxication is a medical emergency; evacuate to professional medical practitioners immediately. A physician may administer an intravenous (IV) solution of physostigmine. If cholinergic effect persists, a second IV is necessary.

Note: This is a favorite hallucinogen, potentially fatal, used by teenagers in some rural areas; a toxic dose varies from plant to plant. The "get high" dose of imbibed seeds is very close to the fatal dose.

DOGBANE, INDIAN HEMP
Apocynaceae (*Apocynum cannabinum*)

Identification: Grows to 6', reddish stems excrete milky latex-like sap when torn or if petioles are broken; broadly lanceolate leaves are opposite, 3"–4" long and 1.5"–2" wide. Entire margins (not toothed), smooth on top with hairs underneath. White flowers bloom in summer and have a 5-lobed corolla with large sepals.

Habitat: Widespread in the northern hemisphere of North America.

Toxins: Cardiac glycosides and a skin-aggravating latex sap.

Symptoms: Overdose of dogbane induces nausea, vomiting, weakness, adominal pain, spasms, and stupor. Milky sap may cause skin blisters.

First Aid: Seek professional medical advice about any treatment. Treatment includes sedation and medical interventions to counteract arrhythmias induced by cardiac glycosides.

Note: Dogbane is easily confused with milkweed when young. The name *dogbane* suggests its toxic capacity to incapacitate dogs. The common name *Indian hemp* refers to use as a fiber and weaving material. The plant is toxic but not psychoactive.

DUTCHMAN'S BREECHES, SQUIRREL CORN

Papaveraceae (*Dicentra cucullaria, D. canadensis*)

Identification: Deeply dissected leaves (lacy looking) without a stalk, and a white flower that looks like a man's breeches. Squirrel corn flower is less breeches-like; that is, less leggy. Underground bulb is scaly. Species are similar, but *D. canadensis* has a fragrant, more heart-shaped flower.

Dicentra cucullaria

Habitat: Habitats overlap for both species. Eastern forested areas, west to the Columbia River basin in Washington. Profuse colonies often found in western mountainous areas.

Toxins: Isoquinoline alkaloids are toxic in large quantities but rarely fatal, although they may cause convulsions. Avoid eating!

Symptoms: May cause skin irritation when touched. Symptoms from ingestion include trembling, a staggering gait, vomiting, diarrhea, convulsions, and labored breathing.

Dicentra canadensis

First Aid: Self-limiting in small doses. Hydrate.

FOXGLOVE, PURPLE FOXGLOVE

Scrophulariaceae (*Digitalis purpurea*)

Identification: Biennial (flowers bloom in summer of second year), 3'–5' tall with lance-shaped, fuzzy, hairy leaves in basal rosette. Hairy basal rosette of leaves looks somewhat like mullein leaves or comfrey leaves, and not like smooth dock leaves—the leaves of digitalis are toxic. Drooping

thimble-shaped flowers on a spike, white to purple or pink; flowers look like gloves, hence the name.

Habitat: Common mountain wildflower, found along roadsides in Northwest and eastern mountain states. This is a favorite ornamental in gardens from coast to coast.

Toxins: Irritating saponins and digitalis glycosides.

Symptoms: Pain in mouth and throat, abdominal pain, nausea, vomiting, cramps, and diarrhea after ingestion. Heart rate accelerates, ventricular thrust increases.

First Aid: This is a medical emergency; evacuate to professional help. Activated charcoal and saline cathartics administered in conjunction with potassium supplementation.

Note: Digitalis glycosides and similar chemistry are used to treat congestive heart failure, resulting in improved cardiac output and an improvement in the signs and symptoms of hemodynamic insufficiency such as edema and/or venous congestion.

HELLEBORE, FALSE HELLEBORE, CALIFORNIA CORN POPPY
Liliaceae (*Veratrum viride*)

Identification: Large, ovate, stalkless leaves, clinging and spiraling up a sturdy stem; yellow-green flower in branched clusters.

Habitat: Grows in wet, swampy areas in the East; found on open mountain slopes and moist areas in the West.

Toxins: Germindine and jervine steroidal alkaloids are potentially fatal if eaten.

Symptoms: Burning mouth, burning throat, excessive salivation, headache, nausea, sweats, diarrhea, accompanied with vomiting with convulsions and delirium.

First Aid: Medical emergency! Hypotension from intoxication requires the use of a dopamine infusion with slow patient improvement; bradycardia and heart blockage persist for up to 2 days.

Note: Interestingly, atropine (which is isolated from datura) has been administered in the last century as a treatment for hellebore poisoning. Hellebore is poisonous to sheep and perhaps other native grazing animals. Chemistry is used as an insecticide; an alcohol infusion of the plant, diluted in water and then strained, is used as a pesticide.

HEMLOCK, POISON
Umbelliferae (*Conium maculatum*)

Identification: Purple-spotted, hollow stems; grows to 6" or 7" with white flowers in umbels that are either flat or umbrella shaped; leaves are divided, parsley-like, into small leaflets (like carrot plant leaves or Queen Anne's lace). Plant has many characteristics of edible members of the parsley family. When crushed, leaves emit a noxious odor.

Habitat: Roadsides and disturbed ground from East to West, north into Canada, and south to New Mexico, but primarily a northern temperate plant in the wild.

Toxins: Ingestion of toxin conine and related alkaloids can be fatal.

Symptoms: Irritation of mucous membranes, mouth, and throat after ingestion, causing salivation, nausea, and emesis. Headache, thirst, and sweating also occur. With severe poisoning, convulsions, coma, and respiratory failure occasionally lead to death.

First Aid: Severe medical emergency! While evacuating administer slurry of activated charcoal after vomiting ceases.

HORSE NETTLE
Solanum (*Solanum carolinense*)

Identification: Thorny plant to 3' tall. Leaves and stems with spines. Coarse, irregular, large-toothed leaves; white flower with yellow reproductive parts.

Habitat: Fields, waste ground, and roadsides from coast to coast.

Toxins: Alkaloid, solanum.

Symptoms: Vomiting, stomach and bowel pain.

First Aid: Fatalities are rare, but aggressive treatment is necessary. Fatal intoxications are more common in children. First aid requires emesis, fluid replacement, and supportive care, including treatment for gastroenteritis.

Note: Toxic berry looks edible, like a small tomato.

JACK-IN-THE-PULPIT

Araceae (*Arisaema triphyllum*)

Identification: Solitary plant, typically with a central flowering stalk. Flower is a spathe and spadix, and with a little imagination, you can see a preacher in a pulpit.

Habitat: Moist woods in the eastern and central United States.

Toxins: Calcium oxalate.

Symptoms: A dangerous and contraceptive herb if not prepared properly, and even at that, not palatable. Burning in mouth and throat; ingestion leads to diarrhea, teary eyes, nausea, vomiting, slurred speech, tongue, and swollen mouth.

First Aid: Do not induce vomiting. Wipe out mouth with a cold, wet cloth. Give the person milk to drink, unless instructed otherwise by professional health-care provider (i.e., no milk if the patient is vomiting or having convulsions, or has any decreased level of alertness that may make it hard to swallow). Evacuate to emergency room for medical help. Stomach may be emptied. With stomach and intestinal involvement, copious amounts of water may be administered. Medications may include diphenhydramine, epinephrine, or famotidine. Treatment is for anaphylactic reaction.

For skin exposure: Wash the skin with water. If the plant material touched the eyes, rinse the eyes with water.

Note: My poisoning with calcium oxalate was painful, causing mouth burn, severe stress, and increased heart rate—much like a panic attack. The doctor told me to drink water and take Mylanta—that worked. Native Americans dried the root, apparently denaturing the oxalate, and then roasted the bulbous growths for food.

LARKSPUR, WESTERN

Ranunculaceae (*Delphinium glaucum*)

Identification: Larkspurs are defined by their small star-shaped blossoms, with 1 sepal and 2 petals forming the characteristic spur. Flowers are arranged along a hairy stem that may grow to about 16". Leaves of a larkspur are deeply lobed and joined at a single point. The leaves may appear hairy as well. Plant to 4', shorter at higher altitudes.

Habitat: Larkspur grows wild in many southern states, western rangelands, and many high-altitude streams and lakes visited by this fly fisherman. *D. glaucum* is most frequently found in moist areas in the mountainous West.

Toxins: Diterpenoid alkaloids typified by methyllycaconitine (MLA) are very poisonous.

Symptoms: Symptoms vary as to amount eaten. Fatal poisoning brings convulsions and paralysis of the respiratory system. Autopsies reveal inflammation and/or congestion of the windpipe, stomach and small intestine bloating (including congestion of the superficial blood vessels), and dark, extremely congested kidneys. Little information on human poisonings; biggest problem is with grazing animals. Larkspur causes burning of the mouth and throat, confusion, dizziness, headaches, and vomiting. In severe poisoning, there is difficulty breathing, then paralysis, followed by convulsions and death from asphyxiation and circulatory failure. However, most victims do recover within 24 hours.

First Aid: There is no antidote for larkspur poisoning. Deaths are rare; the taste is acrid, burning, and unpalatable, so typically not much toxin is consumed.

Note: Larkspur, marketed for the garden, has appealing blossoms and foliage; cultivate with caution if children or pets are likely to frequent the garden.

MAYAPPLE

Berberidaceae (*Podophyllum peltatum*)

Identification: Eastern woodland plant to 2', providing ground cover in a forest. Leaves are large, umbrella-like, and deeply dissected, with a single white flower bearing an edible fruit in July. The plant withers by late summer. All other parts of the plant are toxic.

Habitat: Native to deciduous forests of eastern North America.

Toxins: The rhizome, foliage, and roots are poisonous. Mayapple contains podophyllotoxin, which is cytostatic and used topically in the treatment of viral and genital warts. Podophyllum resin contains at least 16 other active compounds, including picropodophyllin, podophyllic acid, α- and β-peltatins, and quercetin.

Symptoms: Powerful cathartic! Excessive ingestion may lead to coma and death. Podophyllum resin is a drastic cathartic with a marked purging action that is highly irritant to the intestinal mucosa and produces violent peristalsis. Laxative use of peltatins causes colonic irritation and is considered to be unsafe by the FDA. There are less toxic laxatives.

First Aid: Consult a physician or poison center immediately. No specific antidote known. Emesis may be useful during the initial phases of toxicity. The fat-soluble chemistry makes hemodialysis ineffective, but charcoal hemoperfusion has reversed acute symptoms within hours. Remove any irritating (topically administered) resin with petroleum jelly. If eye contact occurs, flush with copious amounts of warm water.

Note: When ripe, the fruit may be eaten judiciously. Etoposide and teniposide from mayapple have shown promise in the treatment of a few types of malignant neoplasms (cancerous growths).

MILKWEED
Asclepiadaceae (*Asclepias syriaca* and other species)

Identification: Stomach-shaped seedpod with seeds in follicles and rows with silky white hairs in between. Large ovate leaves that exude milk-like sap when damaged.

Habitat: Common roadside, waste-ground plant.

Toxins: Milkweed is named for its milky juice, which contains galitoxin, alkaloids, latex, and other complex compounds, including cardiac glycosides. A few species are known to be toxic when an amount equal to 10 percent or more of the animal's body weight is consumed. That's a lot of milkweed.

Symptoms: Overdose of milkweed induces vomiting, weakness, adominal pain, nausea, stupor, and spasms.

First Aid: Seek professional medical advice about any treatment. Treatment includes sedation and medical interventions to counteract arrhythmias induced by cardiac glycosides.

Note: Although flowers and young shoots of *A. syriaca* are edible with careful cooking (see FalconGuides' *Basic Illustrated Edible Wild Plants and Useful Herbs* by Jim Meuninck), there are numerous other safe plant choices without cardiac glycosides. Indigenous people of South America and Africa use arrows poisoned with cardiac glycosides to kill game. Milkweed may also cause mild contact dermatitis. The sole food source of monarch butterfly larvae, milkweed is an attractive and active garden addition. Flowers provide an intoxicating fragrance.

MOONSEED

Menispermaceae
(*Menispermum canadense*)

Identification: Climbing woody vine with green stems, to 33'. Leaves are round or heart shaped with a pointed tip; occasionally they are not round but show 3 shallow palmate lobes (6"–10" wide). Unripe green fruit may be confused with wild grapes—ripe fruit is toxic and red with a moon-shaped crescent on the seed—crescent is indicative; pluck the seed from fruit to discover the crescent.

Habitat: Found in lowlands, waste ground, streams, pond sides, and wetlands of the eastern United States and Canada. Habitat overlaps with wild grape and can be confused with such (check seed for crescent).

Toxins: The fruit of Canada moonseed is poisonous and can be fatal. Taste is terrible, and typically the fruit is quickly spit from the mouth with little or no ingestion. The principal toxins are the bitter alkaloids: dauricine, menispine, and berberine.

Symptoms: Convulsions and any or all of the following: stomach upset, vomiting, watery eyes and nose, gastroenteritis, bloody diarrhea, irritation of mouth and lips, difficulty breathing, trouble swallowing, excess salivation, shock, and possibly death.

First Aid: A medical emergency. Call poison control center and evacuate immediately. The stomach may be emptied.

Note: The Cherokee used the root decoction as a laxative, diuretic, and as treatment for venereal diseases and arthritis.

POKEWEED

Phytolaccaceae (*Phytolacca americana*)

Identification: Ovate leaves, pointed at tip; purple stem when mature; elongated clusters of purple berries. Grows from a large rootstock; stems are thick, hollow, and purple. May grow and spread to 10'.

Habitat: The plant grows in gardens, waste ground, vacant lots, and along the fringes of woods.

Toxins: All parts poisonous, particularly the root. Chemically active substances are phytolaccine, formic acid, tannin, and resinous acid. Toxic components of the plant are saponins.

Symptoms: Eating improperly prepared plant may lead to nausea, vomiting, diarrhea, abdominal cramps, headaches, blurred vision, confusion, dermatitis, dizziness, and weakness. In acute and advanced reactions, convulsions, low blood pressure, rapid heartbeat, blockage of the electrical impulses that stimulate the heart to contract, and death may occur.

First Aid: Mild dose is self-limiting, and symptoms subside within 24 hours. Copious ingestion is a medical emergency—evacuate victim.

Note: Juice from the berries is used by the food industry to make red food coloring. Farmers and dairymen use an alcohol extract or tincture of pokeweed to reduce swelling of cows' udders. Young green leaves are edible after thorough cooking in a change of water and then sautéing; pick before stems turn purple for maximum safety. Laboratory research shows a protein called pokeweed antiviral protein (PAP) has antitumor effects in mice; PAP has also shown action against viruses such as herpes and human immunodeficiency virus. Other studies have suggested that certain formulations of PAP may turn out to be useful against cancer cells dependent on hormones for their growth, as in prostate, breast, and ovarian cancers.

SKUNK CABBAGE

Araceae (*Symplocarpus foetidus, Lysichitum americanus*)

Identification: Large, green, elephant-ear-like leaves are lustrous and waxy in appearance with a "skunky" odor when torn. Flower is an archaic, showy sheath surrounding club-like flower spike (spadix).

Habitat: Both western and eastern species occupy lowlands, bogs, and other wetlands with a covering of trees.

Toxins: Calcium oxalate crystals (raphides); avoid using the fresh parts of this plant as food or medicine.

Symptoms: Burning sensation when eaten raw, but difficult to swallow due to caustic nature of oxalates. If swallowed, breathing and heart rate are typically

affected by pain and panic. Also expect numbness; burning of the tongue, mouth, and lips; swelling of tongue or lips; and gastrointestinal symptoms such as nausea, abdominal pain, and diarrhea.

First Aid: Self-limiting; evacuate to emergency room for medical help. Physician may recommend preparations to sooth the digestive system, such as Mylanta, or stomach may be emptied. With stomach and intestinal involvement, victim should drink copious amounts of water. Administered medications may include diphenhydramine, epinephrine, or famotidine. Treatment is for anaphylactic reaction.

Note: This is a rare endothermic plant that produces heat—one of the first plants to bloom, pushing up through ice and snow and then flowering.

SPURGE, CYPRESS SPURGE

Euphorbiaceae (*Euphorbia cyparissias*)

Identification: European native that escaped to the Americas grows to 12" (plus or minus). Yellow-green petals mature to red or purple late in the season. Like spotted touch-me-nots, seedpods explode and widely disperse

seeds. Adventitous roots with lateral root buds give rise to spreading and expansive colonies. Short narrow leaves are distinctive.

Habitat: Widespread in sandy, gravelly soils. Extensive in grazing areas of cattle and horses, to which it is toxic. Found in southern Michigan along roadside banks. Exists from coast to coast—a noxious weed usurping native habitat—yes, the world is becoming a blend of all things, facilitated by us, of course.

Toxins: Bitter, toxic latex.

Symptoms: Emetic, purgative internal irritant to grazing animals. Chief concern with humans is the irritation the toxic latex has to the eyes, lips, ears, and other external areas.

First Aid: Copious irrigation with water. If ingested and swallowed, call a medical professional or evacuate to emergency medical attention.

Note: Spread of plant controlled by flea beetles and parasitic fungi.

WATER HEMLOCK
Apiaceae or Umbelliferae
(*Cicuta maculata*)

Identification: Tall plant (to 8'). Leaves compound with sharply toothed (serrated) lance-shaped leaflets 2"–4" in length; white umbrella-shaped flower clusters, hollow stems; in many ways similar to poison hemlock in appearance—and dangerously similar to a few of its edible family members. Distinctive is the leaf venation, which terminates at the notch instead of the tip. This venation is indicative.

Habitat: Widely distributed across North America. Found near wetlands, edges of streams, marshes, snow melts, mountain meadows and seeps, and springs.

Water hemlock leaf veins

Toxins: Cicutoxin—one of North America's most toxic plants.

Symptoms: Nausea, increased salivation, and seizures within 15–60 minutes after ingestion, leading to rapid deterioration and too often death.

First Aid: Medical emergency, often fatal without immediate intervention; requires IVs of diazepam or other anticonvulsants. Treat for acidosis and maintain urine flow. Mechanical ventilation and intubation may be necessary. Mental deficits in survivors may be prolonged.

Note: This plant has been confused with other Umbelliferae. Get to know this family (cow parsnip, carrot, parsley, fennel, etc.). Seek out the hemlocks and learn to identify them.

WESTERN SKUNK CABBAGE
Araceae (*Lysichitum americanus*)

Identification: Lowland, wetland dweller grows in colonies; has large yellow flower, leaves up to 3' with waxy sheen.

Habitat: Spreading colonial plant in wet areas under western coniferous forests.

Eastern skunk cabbage

Toxins: Contains caustic oxalate crystals.

Symptoms: Burning sensation when eaten raw. If swallowed, breathing and heart rate effected by pain and panic. Also expect numbness; burning of the tongue, mouth, and lips; swelling of tongue or lips; and gastrointestinal symptoms, such as nausea, abdominal pain, and diarrhea.

Western skunk cabbage

First Aid: Evacuate to emergency room for medical help. Stomach may be emptied. With stomach and intestinal involvement, administer copious amounts of water. Administered medications may include diphenhydramine, epinephrine, or famotidine. Treatment is for anaphylactic reaction.

Note: Drying the leaves or roots of Western or Eastern skunk cabbage eliminates some of the peppery, hot taste of the calcium oxalate crystals. Native Americans and other savvy chefs wrap leaves of the Western variety around salmon and pit roast. Cooking does not impart toxic effect.

VETCH, CROWN; AXSEED
Fabaceae (*Coronillia varia, Vinca* species)

Identification: Low-lying, spreading plant to 2'—a ground-covering plant, with pinnate, compound leaves that terminate in tendrils and small, variously colored flowers (but typically blue). Pea- or bean-like seed.

Habitat: Vacant lots, roadsides, abandoned mining sites (as

Vinca *species*

restoring cover), meadows, and other dry areas or areas of poor soil.

Toxins: All parts of crown vetch are toxic. Because of its bean-like fruit, children and animals can accidentally ingest this invasive plant. A toxic constituent of crown vetch is the nitrotoxin, ß-nitropropionic acid, a potent neurotoxin.

Symptoms: Consumed in large amounts, it can slow growth and induce paralysis, or even death.

First Aid: A medical professional may induce vomiting to reduce the amount of toxin in the victim. Learn to identify the plant. Be careful when choosing pea-family foods in the wild—many are potentially toxic; others are delicious. Use a field guide and forage with an expert.

Note: Although animals astutely avoid crown vetch foliage, several sources suggest that seeds are distributed from place to place by ungulates.

YAUPON, YAUPON HOLLY

Aquifoliaceae (*Ilex vomitoria*)
Identification: Yaupon is an evergreen holly, shrub-like with glossy green leaves that have sharp points. Leaves are alternate, simple, shallow toothed. Shrub exhibits small white flowers that produce red berries.

Habitat: Coastal plant typically found in Texas and throughout the Southwest—widely cultivated.

Toxins: Berries are inedible and toxic, containing illicin, saponic glycosides, and triterpenoids.

Symptoms: Mild toxicity exhibiting nausea, vomiting, and diarrhea.

First Aid: Illness follows course and is self-limiting.

Note: Leaves and berries are used to make dyes. The ripe red berries make a red dye in a mordant of alum. Use it on wool—place the wool item in the dye and let the color infuse in full sunlight. Achieve gray color by pounding leaves in water with iron and/or copper. Young leaves may be eaten and/or made into tea.

Chapter Two

Plant Dermatitis

Numerous plants cause inflammatory dermatitis. Protective mechanisms such as exuding chemicals, stiff hairs, stinging cells, and spines protect plants but are hazards in the bush and around the home. Here are several plants best identified and then left alone. Their intention is survival; they are not malicious, but a knowledgeable wilderness traveler respects their rights while being awed by their beauty.

ANGELICA
Umbelliferae (*Angelica atropurpurea, A. sinensis*)

Identification: *A. atropurpurea* is a tall biennial to 9' having a thick, erect purple stem. Large cleft, compound leaves are divided into 3–5 leaflets with hollow petioles. Upper leaves are sheathed as they emerge; sheath remains around the petioles. Greenish-white flowers are in umbrella-like clusters.

Habitat: Found in wet lowlands and along streams and rivers in the northern tier of states, typically east of the Mississippi.

Toxins/Irritants: Psoralens (furanocoumarins)

Symptoms: Phototoxic reaction causing severe burn, inflammation, and consequent pain.

First Aid: Avoid contact with plant leaves and juices. After contact with plant juice, or if plant parts have been eaten, stay out of the sun for 24 hours.

Notes: Like other Umbelliferae, angelica has calcium channel blockers, similar to the drugs used to treat angina, which improve peripheral circulation. Many other Umbelliferae, including carrot, Queen Anne's lace (wild carrot), celery, and parsley, cause contact dermatitis or are phytophototoxic in susceptible individuals. Susceptible people should garden with gloves, long-sleeved shirts, and pants. Native Americans used *A. atropurpurea* root decoctions to treat rheumatism, chills and fevers, flatulence, and as a gargle for sore throat. The plant also was used in sweat lodges to treat arthritis, headaches, frostbite, and hypothermia. Externally, the root can be smashed and applied as a poultice to relieve pain (stay out of the sun). While hiking I have made casual contact with both this plant and cow parsnip without incident. Although angelica is prescribed for psoriasis, I have had no luck with it. The idea is to eat angelica, thereby ingesting psoralens, increasing your sensitivity to UV light. After spending 10 minutes in the sun, the UV-light/psoralen interaction may stop or slow cell division in the skin. Self-administering psoralens and subsequent exposure to light can be phototoxic and carcinogenic. See herbvideos.com for an effective and benign wash for psoriasis. Roots used as a flavoring agent for vodka, gin, cooked fish, and various jams.

COW PARSNIP
Umbelliferae (*Heracleum lanatum*)

Identification: Similar in appearance to angelica and several other members of the carrot family, with large umbels of white flowers and large, deeply cut leaves; hollow stem. Odorous plant to 7' tall, typically smaller in the West.

Habitat: Wetlands, streamsides, and lakesides east and west of the Mississippi; also prevalent along rivers, streams, and trails in the Mountain West.

Toxins/Irritants: Psoralen (furanocoumarins).

Symptoms: Rash, inflammation, and blisters.

First Aid: Avoidance. Learn to identify and avoid contact with juices. In most cases, casual contact while hiking will not produce symptoms. Rash may persist for weeks and months.

Note: An edible stem with skin removed, raw, cooked, or candied. Boiled roots said to clear flatulence. Fresh root said to be an effective poultice: Pound the root and apply. Chemical constitutes linked to cancer in vitro and in vivo studies.

DEVIL'S CLUB
Araliaceae (*Oplopanax horridus*)

Identification: Shrubby perennial to 10', a twisted tangle of spiny thorns. Emits a sweet odor and displays large maple-like leaves armed on the underside with thorns. White flowers grouped in a club-like terminal head.

Habitat: Western mountains to the West Coast, especially in wet areas: seeps, stream banks, moist, low-lying forests— prevalent in the Olympic Range and Cascades, from sea level to the tree line in Canada.

Toxins/Irritants: Damage from this plant is mechanical. Large thorns tear and pierce the skin. Berries are inedible.

Symptoms: Painful puncture wounds that may cause dermatitis in some individuals.

First Aid: Cleanse wounds and, where severe, treat with triple antibiotic ointment.

Note: Spring buds are eaten as a survival food (keep in mind, however, in hard times people will eat dirt, too). Look for them early, right after the snow melts, and pick young shoots with soft spines. This armored plant walls off every environment where it thrives. One of the most important medicinal plants of the West; its roots, berries, and greenish bark are used. Berries are rubbed in hair to kill lice and create a shine. Inner bark is chewed raw as a purgative, or decocted and imbibed for the same reason. Infused inner bark is taken to relieve bowel and stomach cramps, arthritis, and ulcers. For further reference, see the author's *Basic Illustrated Edible Wild Plants and Useful Herbs* or visit his website, herbvideos.com.

HOGWEED, GIANT HOGWEED
Umbelliferae (*Heracleum mantegazzianum*)

Identification: Similar in appearance to cow parsnip, but typically much larger (to 12') with more deeply cleft leaves, white flowers, and hollow stem.

Habitat: Plant of wetlands, streamsides, and lakesides east and west of the Mississippi. Prevalent on waste ground. An invasive alien from the Far East.

Toxins/Irritants: Psoralen (furanocoumarins).

Symptoms: Rash, inflammation, and blisters more severe than either cow parsnip or other Umbelliferae—a plant that must be avoided and, according to many, eradicated. Personally it's a striking plant; it's here, like us, therefore enjoy its natural beauty but beware of its sinister effects that can last for months, even years.

First Aid: Avoidance. Learn to identify and avoid contact with juices.

Note: This plant is hyped as a bad actor, but it can't walk and does not strike with fangs. It punishes those who fail to identify it and then come in contact with its juices, so be careful.

HOPS
Cannabaceae (*Humulus lupulus*)

Identification: Climbing perennial with pencil-thick stems that do not turn woody. The plant climbs through shrubs and spreads. Leaves are opposite, 3–5 lobed, and serrated. Male flowers are yellowish green, small, and inconspicuous. Female flowers have numerous florets, and a fruit cone grows from the flowers. Cone may be yellowish to gray, depending on whether it is fresh or dried. The scales of the cone contain the bitter alkaloid.

Habitat: Plant has escaped from cultivation and can be found in marshes, meadows, and the edges of woods. Cultivated stands are in northeastern Washington State, east of Seattle in the Okanagon of Washington, in northern Idaho, and Canada.

Toxins/Irritants: Contact with hops, the pollen and leaves, has caused allergic reactions. Fertilizers and pesticides have been eliminated as the cause—the dermatitis is caused by the plant and in a few cases a bacterium present on the plant (*Pantoea agglomerans*). Allergy sensitive individuals show positive reactions to various hop oils and acids.

Symptoms: Contact dermatitis. Work hazard for cultivators and harvesters of the crop for the beer-brewing industry; also a dermatitis hazard in breweries. Of interest, water-soluble extract of hops has inhibited ovulation in rats. Allergy typically expressed as small oozing papules and vesicles on the sides of fingers.

First Aid: Avoid contact, wear mask and gloves, long sleeves. Condition is self-limiting.

Notes: Early research suggested that the flower tea may impart estrogenic effect; subsequent research has not shown this. German Commission E approved for treating nervousness and insomnia (sleep aid). The flavonoids in the plant in animal and in vitro studies show them to be antibacterial, antifungal, and antitumor. Like so many plant teas, it is a diuretic. In mouse studies humulon reduced the average number of tumors in cancer-induced mice. In another human study, hops, combined with valerian, balm, and motherwort, improved sleep in alcoholics. In other research, the University of Chicago is completing a study of hops as a sleep aid effective in inducing sleep. For those allergic to hops, related research suggests that the use of melatonin is a relatively safe alternative. For a relaxing steam bath, place hops in a clean pair of panty hose, tie off, and put in hot bath water. Or make a sweat lodge from a dome tent, cover the tent with a tarp and a blanket, and then heat stones over an outside fire until hot; place stones in a large 5-gallon enameled metal container and transfer to the floor of the tent. Place the metal tub on boards so as not to burn the tent floor. Drop water-soaked cedar boughs and hops on the hot stones, and use a long-handled ladle to dip water carefully over the rocks. The resultant steam will warm the lodge with healing aromatics. According to some sources smoking hops may provide a mild sedative effect. To make a sleep aid, add about 1 teaspoon of dried flowers to a 6-ounce cup of hot water, just off the boil. Cover, cool, and drink.

POISON IVY

Anacardiaceae (*Toxicodendron radicans*)

Identification: Climbing hairy vine or shrub, leaflets in threes, with white or pale-yellow berries. Vine clings to trees with hairs.

Habitat: Woods, waste ground, dunes, fields, fence rows—about anywhere, coast to coast, north to south.

Toxins/Irritants: Oily resin called urushiol.

Symptoms: Contact dermatitis—inflammation, reddening, blistering, itching—may persist for days.

First Aid: With inflammation on your face, stay out of the sun. Rub with jewelweed (spotted touch-me-nots) to reduce redness and itching. Numerous medical treatments include calamine lotion, steroid-free TriCalm, Zanfel wash, and corticosteroids such as prednisone. Typically, the dermatitis is self-limiting and clears in 2 weeks or less.

Note: A thorough scrubbing with soap and water within an hour of contact often prevents this rash and associated discomfort.

POISON OAK

Anacardiaceae (*Toxicodendron diversiloba*)

Identification: A small shrub, resembles poison ivy but with more deeply cleft lobes. Leaves are shiny, stemless, and hairy.

Habitat: Often found in the West, mountain valleys and canyons of California. Also an Eastern variety.

Toxins/Irritants: Urushiol.

Symptoms: Causes contact dermatitis, rash, itching.

First Aid: Similar to poison ivy and poison sumac; treat with Benadryl, calamine lotion, oatmeal baths; in severe cases prednisone and other anti-inflammatory steroids, either over-the-counter or prescription, are used.

POISON SUMAC
Anacardiaceae *(Rhus vernix)*

Identification: Shrub to 10' with compound leaves, 7–15 leaflets with white fruit (berries dangling from delicate stems).

Habitat: Wetlands, bogs, marshes, and hemlock forests of the eastern United States.

Toxins/Irritants: Urushiol.

Symptoms: Causes contact dermatitis, itching, blistering, inflammation, and symptoms similar to poison ivy and poison sumac.

First Aid: Thoroughly wash skin with soap and water immediately (up to an hour, even 2 hours) after exposure, which removes the oils before they penetrate the skin. The oil remains on clothing and other objects up to a year, so wash all clothing and tools thoroughly. Oatmeal and/or baking soda baths using tepid, not hot, water can also decrease itching. Calamine lotion topically applied to lesions helps dry them and decreases the itching. Creams containing hydrocortisone, a steroid that reduces inflammation and can decrease itching, are available over the counter. Prescription steroid creams have a higher concentration of hydrocortisone and are also effective.

Note: While hiking I once inadvertently broke off a branch of poison sumac and used it as a staff. It was disheartening and amazing how much of my body was covered with the rash the next day after the hike.

STINGING NETTLE
Urticacea (*Urtica dioica*)

Identification: Erect, tall, and square perennial plant; grooved stem studded with stinging hairs; leaves dark green, rough, heart to oval shaped, toothed; green flowers born in leaf axils, bearing numerous green seeds. Both sexes on one plant and a few plants with separate sexes.

Habitat: Edges of fields, streamsides, wetlands, marshy areas, fringe areas, wasteland, and roadsides nationwide.

Toxins/Irritants: Formic acid, histamine, choline, acetylcholine.

Symptoms: Immediate burning, itching rash when in contact with stinging hairs.

First Aid: Self-limiting; a few people are more susceptible than others. Rubbing with mullein leaf or the application of the juice from spotted touch-me-nots (jewelweed, *Impatiens capensis*) is effective—simply crush the leaves and stems and rub over rash.

Note: Counterirritant; nettles are used to thrash arthritic joints. Whipping the arthritic area causes pain and inflammation, bringing temporary relief—not recommended. Commission E approved it for treating benign prostatic hyperplasia (BPH). Nettle root and saw palmetto have been combined successfully to treat prostate enlargement symptoms. Tincture of nettle roots (soaked and processed in alcohol) in Russia has been administered for hepatitis and gall bladder inflammation. Nettle root extract has been researched for the treatment of prostate hyperplasia in the United States as well.

TANSY

Asteraceae (*Tanacetum vulgare*)

Identification: Plant stem is tough, erect, reddish, and smooth, with branches typically near the top. Leaves are alternate, compound, and feathery pinnate (finely divided), fernlike, with toothed edges. Numerous flower heads are in terminal clusters; flower looks like round yellow buttons with dense, flattish heads. Aromatic plant.

Habitat: Found nationwide near water, along stream banks, ponds, lakes, rivers. There is a large stand in Paradise Valley at Loch Leven Campground on the bank of the Yellowstone River, Montana. It is a dominant herb at Sandy Point, Washington. And we have more than enough here in Michigan.

Toxins/Irritants: The monoterpene ketone thujone.

Symptoms: Excessive consumption of thujone leads to convulsions with brain and liver damage.

First Aid: Identify and avoid the plant. Liver transplant is not the way to go.

Note: This plant has spread from coast to coast. It is colonial and spreads by adventitious roots—tough to eradicate. The tansy beetle is unaffected by thujone and thrives almost exclusively on tansy. Thujone is contained in numerous plants (absinthe for example) and comes prepared in beverages in amounts controlled by statutes—best to avoid it.

WOOD NETTLE
Urticaceae (*Laportea canadensis*)

Identification: Typically a woodland plant with stinging hairs, similar to stinging nettle but with serrated ovate leaves (more oval and paler than nettle) that are opposite and heart shaped at base, with loose clusters of small green flowers in the upper axils of the leaves; female flowers higher, male flowers lower in shorter clusters; crescent-shaped fruit; plant grows to 4'.

Habitat: Eastern woodlands and preferably moist woodlands, often in large colonies.

Toxins/Irritants: Formic acid, histamine, ascorbic acid, choline, acetylcholine.

Symptoms: Itching, burning, stinging; inflammation more severe than stinging nettle and longer lasting.

First Aid: Rub with jewelweed (*Impatiens capensis*), which is typically found nearby. Cold water provides relief. Irritation is self-limiting. Avoid scratching and keep a stiff upper lip.

Note: Wear long pants in woods heralding this plant, and a long-sleeved shirt, too—easily identified, easily avoided.

Chapter Three

Allergic Rhinitis

This section identifies plants that trigger allergies. The main culprits in the inflammatory reaction called pollinosis or allergic rhinitis are dull-colored flowers that are wind-pollinated, including trees and grasses. This condition is also known to many as hay fever, because it becomes most severe during the traditional hay-mowing season. Although numerous grass pollens initiate pollinosis, pine pollen, weed pollen, and any other wind-pollinated plants also may be indicated: alder, birch, chestnut, hazelnut, hornbeam, horse chestnut, and a variety of olives—silverberry, buffalo berry, and Russian olive. Pinecones produce a prodigious amount of pollen that saturates Rocky Mountain air through late June and early July. Also, a few poplars and linden are indicated as culprits. Of note, insect-pollinated plants are often confused as allergenic, but due to the large size of their pollen, they do not become airborne and therefore are not inhaled.

More broadly, allergic rhinitis inflames the nasal air passages of individuals sensitized to an allergen such as pollen, mites, foreign particles in dust, and animal dander. When inhaled, the allergen triggers the immune system to release antibody immunoglobulin E that binds to mast cells and basophils, triggering the release of histamine and other inflammatory agents that cause swelling of the nasal passages, mucus production, watery eyes, sneezing, and itching—and in severe cases rashes and hives. Statistics suggest three out of four people will experience an allergic reaction of some kind in their lifetime, and as many as one in four people have allergic rhinitis. Tests for allergens include patch, scratch (skin prick), intradermal, and other tests, including the radioallergosorbent test (RAST), a blood test. These tests help identify the specific allergen, or in many cases, several allergens.

Pollinosis may be seasonal or last throughout the year. It may be mild, moderate-intermittent, severe-intermittent, or even persistent. Persistent rhinitis is defined by episodes more than four days per week and for more than four weeks.

Symptoms: The spectrum of symptoms includes watery eyes, excessive mucus, nasal congestion (swelling and inflammation), swollen eyelids, rings under the eyes, and pressure in the middle ear. In some cases, an allergenic plant may cause itching in the throat when eaten. In my case, eating spotted touch-me-nots (jewelweed, *Impatiens capensis*) triggers throat itching. If a plant causes this symptom, do not eat it.

First Aid: To prevent or reduce symptoms, prescribed intranasal corticosteroids can be effective without oral antihistamines. Be patient; effectiveness of steroid sprays improves over time. Oral prednisone and triamcinolone acetonide injections are sometimes used, but they are limited by side effects and short duration of efficacy. Next-generation antihistamines reduce symptoms without drowsiness. Nasal irrigation is adjunct therapy. Desensitization therapy requires administering an allergen in increasing doses over a long period of time. This treatment, called allergen immunotherapy, may take over a year to show results—and is sometimes ineffective. New therapies emerge almost daily; consult your physician, take a test, and initiate treatment.

RAGWEED, BITTERWEED, BLOODWEED

Asteraceae (*Ambrosia artemisiifolia,* and other species)

Identification: Tall, tough, erect plant growing to 6' in height, some species smaller; stems basally branched; leaves gray to silver green, lobed with winged petioles; some species have simple leaves. Leaves start out opposite near base and become alternate higher up the plant. They may multiply adventitiously with a creeping rhizome extending from the taproot. Female and male flowering heads are separate on the same plant; yellow-green male flowers on a terminal spike with inconspicuous, whitish-green female flowers situated in leaf axils below male flowers' spikes. The wind-pollinated female flower develops into a prickly burr containing one arrowhead-shaped seed. Wayfaring animals disperse the clinging seeds.

Habitat: Found on waste ground, along roadsides, edges of fields, fringes of wetlands, and in vacant lots and sandy soils. Plant is drought tolerant.

Toxins/Allergen: Amb a 1, a non-glycosylated protein on the pollen considered the most allergenic by many, is present on billions of ragweed pollen, the amount produced from a single plant. Profilin and other calcium-binding allergenic proteins are also present. With climate change and human dispersal and the consequent disruption of topography by such, ragweed has spread to virgin areas where it is not native. Thus, escaping ragweed hay fever by heading for the mountains or the Southwest is no longer a sure thing.

Symptoms: Classic hay fever, allergic rhinitis.

First Aid: See your physician. If suffering, test for allergies. Identify the culprit(s) and take steps toward relief as described in the introduction to this section.

Note: Ragweed pollen has been found in wild raw honey. Skin contact with plant juices and pollen may induce allergies. The weed is difficult to eradicate. The sooner you get to pulling it, the better. Don't let it get a big footprint on your property; stay on top of it. The plant does, however, have a purpose. Ragweed seeds are food for rabbits, doves, voles, grasshoppers, juncos, quail, finch, and red bellied woodpeckers. It is a pre-Columbian food stuff utilized by

Native Americans in lieu of corn. This antique vegetable's seed is 47 percent crude protein and 38 percent crude fat. In Europe, it is a favored food for sheep. In the garden it is a companion to peppers drawing away destructive insects. And along roadsides it scrubs lead from the soil—yes, indeed, a very hardworking member of Earth's family.

GOLDENROD
Asteraceae (*Solidago canadensis; Solidago* spp.)

Identification: Perennial with numerous species. *S. canadensis,* the most common eastern species, has a smooth stem at the base but gets hairy just below flower branches. Sharp-toothed leaves are plentiful, lance shaped with 3 veins. Golden flowers line up atop the stem in a broad, branched spire blooming from bottom to top forming a triangle-shaped cluster (panicle). Plant found most often in colonies. Flowers from July through September.

Habitat: Nationwide fields, meadows, roadsides, stream banks, railroad rights-of-way, vacant lots, edges of fields.

Toxins/Allergen: Goldenrod is mistaken as the weed that causes autumn allergies—that's ragweed. But according to the *PDR for Herbal Medicine* (3rd ed.), the European goldenrod (*Solidago virgaurea*) pollen "has a weak potential" as an allergen.

Notes: Informants say goldenrod floral tea (fresh or dried) may protect a person from allergens (hypoallergenic). So it depends on the individual. The plant has, however, a carbon-to-nitrogen ratio that is tilted toward carbon—providing grasshoppers and other goldenrod insect pollinators with the increased carbohydrates they require. Seeds, shoots, and leaves are edible. Flowers can be made into a mild tea or used as a garnish on salads and other cold or hot dishes. Dried leaves and flowers applied to wounds are styptic. Traditional herbalists and pioneers used the tea to ward off acute infections like colds, flu, and bronchitis—it induces the production of mucus. Diuretic whole-plant tea is a kidney tonic. German Commission E approved *S. virgaurea* for treatment of kidney and bladder stones as well as urinary tract infections. Plants gathered when in flower and dried are used in Europe as a spasmolytic (relaxant) and anti-inflammatory. The drug is prepared 6 to 12 g dried aerial parts in infusion. People with kidney and bladder problems should only use the herb under medical supervision. Also, the whole plant is used as a yellow dye.

Goldenrod nectar and pollen attracts bees, butterflies, wasps, moths, flies, caterpillars, aphids, and other small insects that eat the leaves and stems; wasps, spiders, praying mantises, lacewings, ambush bugs, assassin bugs, beetles, and birds prey on these feasting insects. There is a goldenrod spider that inhabits the plants. Gallflies lay eggs in the stems and leaves. Insect-devouring praying mantises lay their eggs on goldenrod because of its insect-attracting power.

PINE, WHITE PINE, PINYON PINE, LODGEPOLE PINE, PONDEROSA PINE

Pinacea (*Pinus* spp.)

Identification: Coniferous evergreen species, often resin producing, growing from 3'–270' in height. Bark, in most cases, is thick and scaly; branches rise up tree in a tight spiral, appearing as whorls around the trunk. Produces pinecones that yield prodigious amounts of windblown pollen.

Habitat: Native to most biomes in the Northern Hemisphere and widely introduced in tropical and subtropical areas. Trees are widespread in mountains, wetlands, and elsewhere in near desert conditions.

Toxins/Allergen: Allergy-producing pollen proteins.

Symptoms: Allergic rhinitis, including sinus congestion, nasal drip.

First Aid: With pine pollen, I have found that nasal-sinus irrigation is helpful. Do it twice a day for 2 days, and then once a day until symptoms diminish. For acute conditions use standard therapies described in the introduction to this section.

Note: In late June and the first few days of July lodgepole pines produce copious clouds of pollen in the Absaroka-Beartooth Wilderness, Montana. People with pine-pollen allergies are typically allergic to grass pollen.

Chapter Four

Toxic Houseplants

This chapter identifies houseplants that pose potential threats to you, your children, friends, and pets. If you cannot identify any suspected poisonous plant, call your local extension center or home and garden education center for assistance. Online there are many sites that list potentially dangerous houseplants; use this field guide and the resource supplement at the end of this book. It is also important to realize that many plants must be consumed in considerable quantities for systemic poisoning to occur. Often poisonous plants taste bitter or acrid, or they may sting the tongue, preventing children and pets from ingesting large amounts. Teach young children not to touch or put unknown plants or plant parts in their mouths.

If a child or pet ingests a houseplant or dried decoration and poisoning is suspected, call your family doctor, nearest emergency room, or veterinarian immediately. The number for the American Association of Poison Control Centers is (800) 222-1222. They can tell you if a plant is poisonous and what symptoms to expect with a particular toxin. You will need to provide them with the identity of the plant, however.

Be prepared to give the patient's age, weight, and symptoms. Try to discover and relate the parts of the plant eaten, the amount swallowed, and when.

What follows are the most toxic common in-home plants and important points to know before calling for emergency help.

ALOE VERA, ALOE BARBADENSIS

Liliaceae (*Aloe vera syn. Aloe barbadensis*)

Identification: The leaves are thick and fleshy, green to gray-green. A few varieties display white flecks on the upper and lower stem surfaces. The margin of the leaf is serrated with small white teeth. Flowers are on a spike up to 36" tall, florets are pendulous with a yellow tubular corolla. Plant is widely available for purchase.

Habitat: Found in the wild across North Africa, the Canary Islands, and the Arabian peninsula and cultivated throughout the world.

Toxins: Latex, aloe-emodin, aloin, and barbaloin.

Symptoms: Contact dermatitis can occur in sensitive individuals. Latex is cathartic and irritating to digestive tract.

First Aid: Wash skin irritant with tepid water. Cathartic effect is self-limiting; replace fluids.

Note: Aloe, a healing plant used for burns, cuts, and other skin problems, helps to remove formaldehyde from indoor air. Whole leaf consumption by rats induced tumors.

CYCLAMEN, SOWBREAD, PERSIAN VIOLET

Myrsinaceae (*Cyclamen* spp.)

Identification: Ornamental flowers with upswept petals and variably patterned leaves. Flowers and roots grow from a tuber, which is round and develops from the stem of a seedling. Often mistakenly called a corm, but a corm (in crocuses for example) has a papery tunic and a basal plate from which the roots grow. The

storage organ of the cyclamen has no papery covering, and roots may grow out of any part.

Habitat: Native to the Mediterranean and northeastern Africa.

Toxins: Tuber, rhizomes contain cyclamin A.

Symptoms: Strong purgative (diarrhea) reaction to eating tubers or rhizomes.

First Aid: Self-limiting. Rehydrate.

Note: A hardy indoor plant that will survive some neglect and provide exotic beauty throughout the year.

DEVIL'S BACKBONE, MOTHER OF THOUSANDS
Euphorbiaceae (*Kalanchoe daigremontian*)

Identification: Unusual succulent with young "plantlets" growing along the leaf edges. Plantlets easily dislodge and fall in profusion around the base of the adult.

Habitat: Native to Madagascar.

Toxins: Daigremontianin (cardiac glycoside) in leaves, plantlets, and stems.

Symptoms: Little documentation but with a large ingestion, scenario may include nausea, vomiting, cramping, diarrhea, oral pain with sinus bradycardia lowering heart rate to 50–60 beats that may cause cardiac arrest because of insufficient oxygen to the heart.

First Aid: Moderate to extreme intoxication is a medical emergency. Evacuate. Physician may administer gastric lavage or induce vomiting, with administration of activated charcoal as necessary.

Note: Children and family pets have easy access to fallen toxic plantlets—also toxic to chicks and mice.

HEART-LEAF PHILODENDRON, LACE TREE PHILODENDRON
Araceae (*Philodendron* spp.)

Identification: Climbing vines with aerial roots. Two varieties exhibit different large, heart-shaped leaves: either entire or irregularly notched.

Habitat: Subtropical and tropical in wild. Found in profusion in Baja Mexico as an ornamental. One of the most popular ornamental indoor houseplants in the United States.

Toxins: Calcium oxalate in leaves and stems.

Symptoms: General symptoms of contact dermatitis with the plant juices are erythema (reddening and inflammation of the skin) and itchiness. Ingestion will quickly cause painful burning and swelling of lips, mouth, tongue, and throat.

First Aid: Rinse eyes with copious amount of water. Skin contact with oxalates requires copious water irrigation, although the irritant is more soluble in vinegar. For oral exposures, physically remove any plant material from the mouth and check if airway is compromised; if not, ingest cold liquids, ice cream, Popsicles, or crushed ice for relief, or take analgesics. A physician may administer via mouth diphenhydramine elixir, providing local anesthetic and antihistaminic effects. Compromised airway treatment requires antihistamines, hospitalization, and observation until the edema improves; typically oral edema. A physician may recommend digestive-system-soothing preparations such as Mylanta. For a large dose or allergic

reaction, stomach may be emptied and victim administered copious amounts of water. Medications may include diphenhydramine, epinephrine, or famotidine. Treatment is for anaphylactic reaction.

Note: Philodendrons were among the best houseplants in NASA's tests for removing toxins from indoor air.

KAFFIR LILY

Amaryllidaceae (*Clivia miniata*)

Identification: Strap-like leaves from swollen leaf base in opposite piles. Kaffirs produce a cluster (umbel) of tubular orange flowers with yellow throats. Fruit is a cherry-size green berry that eventually turns to a pulpy red berry.

Habitat: Native to Africa, cultivated houseplant.

Toxins: Kaffir lily roots contain small amounts of the alkaloid lycorine. Large quantities must be ingested to cause symptoms.

Symptoms: Diarrhea, salivation, vomiting, paralysis, collapse.

First Aid: Serious poisoning is rare. Fluid replacement is necessary if dehydration occurs or is imminent.

MOTHER-IN-LAW'S TONGUE, SNAKE PLANT, DIEFFENBACHIA

Araceae (*Dieffenbachia spp.*)

Identification: Houseplant with tall, colorful, elongated, blade-shaped leaves that are unbranched and grow in dense, tightly bundled colonies.

Habitat: Subtropical to tropical plant has escaped to numerous areas, native to southern Mexico and Central America; a common houseplant.

Toxins: All parts contain calcium oxalate raphides; also, asparagine.

Symptoms: Painful swelling of the mouth and throat after ingesting leaf may result in speech impediment that can last for several days. Raphides burn and stab on their way down. Eye contact with the juices causes pain and swelling.

First Aid: Check if airway is compromised; if not, ingest cold liquids, ice cream, Popsicles, or crushed ice for relief. Take analgesic if necessary. A physician may administer diphenhydramine elixir via mouth, providing local anesthetic and antihistaminic effects. Rinse eyes with copious amounts of water. Compromised airway treatment requires antihistamines, hospitalization, and observation until the edema improves. Skin contact with oxalates requires water irrigation, although the irritant is more soluble in vinegar. For oral exposures, physically remove any plant material from the mouth; typically, oral edema presents. Attending physician may recommend digestive-system-soothing preparations such as Mylanta. For large dose or allergic reaction, evacuate to emergency medical help. With stomach and intestinal involvement, stomach may be emptied and the victim administered copious amounts of water. Administered medications may include epinephrine, or famotidine. Treatment is for anaphylactic reaction. For incidental exposure in mouth, on lips, or on skin, wipe out the mouth (or other exposed area) with a cold, wet cloth. Apply copious water to rinse the eyes and skin. Drink milk and call your local emergency number (such as 911) or the American Association of Poison Control Centers at (800) 222-1222.

Note: Other houseplants from Areceae family containing calcium oxalates include caladium (*Caladium hortulanum*) and the flamingo lily (*Anthurium sp.*).

PEACE LILY

Araceae (*Spathiphyllum* spp.)

Identification: Evergreen, herbaceous plant with large leaves having a greenish spadix surrounded by a white, green, or yellow spathe—a shade plant that is drought tolerant.

Habitat: Tropics of Americas and Southeast Asia, shade-loving understory plant.

Toxins: Calcium oxalate raphides (sharp crystals).

Symptoms: Chewing induces intense needle-piercing pain. External skin irritant. Large ingestion is a medical emergency: nausea, diarrhea, tachycardia, burning sensation in mouth and intestines. See mother-in-law's tongue (snake plant, dieffenbachia).

First Aid: Irrigate external exposure with copious amounts of tepid water. If severe, evacuate to emergency room for medical help. With stomach and intestinal involvement, administer copious amounts of water. Administered medications may include diphenhydramine, epinephrine, or famotidine. Treatment is for anaphylactic reaction. A physician may recommend digestive-system-soothing preparations such as Mylanta. Not a systemic toxin in humans.

Note: Excellent air-cleaning houseplant; water weekly, tolerates shade and neglect. *Spathiphyllum* is mildly toxic to animals when ingested. The peace lily is not a true lily of the Liliaceae family. True lilies, including onions and garlic, are much more toxic to cats and dogs—causing skin irritation, burning sensation in the mouth, difficulty swallowing, and nausea.

POTHOS, GOLDEN POTHOS

Araceae (*Epipremnum aureum*)

Identification: Tropical evergreen vine to 70' that climbs by means of aerial roots that adhere to structures and surfaces. Leaves are alternate, heart shaped, entire on juvenile plants but irregular on mature plants; very large on wild plants, smaller on indoor cultivars. Flowers to 9" in length, seeds produced in a spadix partially surrounded by a primitive spathe.

Habitat: Native range extends from northern Australia, Malaysia, southern China, southern Japan, and India—an invasive species in subtropical and tropical areas worldwide.

Toxins: Calcium oxalate rhaphides.

Symptoms: Most toxic to domestic animals and children. Insoluble raphides feel like sharp needles in the mouth, causing pain, oral irritation, vomiting, and difficulty swallowing.

First Aid: If severe, evacuate to emergency room for medical help. With stomach and intestinal involvement, victim drinks copious amounts of water. Administered medications may include diphenhydramine, epinephrine, or famotidine. Treatment is for anaphylactic reaction.

Note: This plant is often placed in aquariums and around the edges of ponds in warmer climates. The root and rootlets will grow through stone or gravel gardens, seeking moisture, absorbing nitrates, and cleansing the water.

Chapter Five

Toxic Garden Plants

Gardeners, be aware of the potential problems with plants that have toxic properties. Instruct children to avoid eating garden plants and wild plants without your okay and under your supervision.

AMARYLLIS, JERSEY LILY, LILY LANGTRY

Amaryllidaceae (*Amaryllis* sp.)

SHUTTERSTOCK.COM

Identification: Green strap-shaped leaves emerge from the bulb in the autumn, and give way the following year to 1 or 2 leafless flower bearing stems (up to 25" tall) each of which bears a cluster of 2–12 funnel-shaped flowers at their tips. Each flower is 3"–4" in diameter with 6 sepals (3 outer sepals and 3 inner petals similar in appearance). Flower color is white with crimson veins (bright red), but varieties may show pink or purple naturally.

Habitat: Native to South Africa; cultivated worldwide.

Toxins: Bulb contains small amounts of lycorine, thus eating large quantities of the bulb cause symptoms.

Symptoms: Diarrhea, nausea, vomiting.

First Aid: Rare intoxication because amounts eaten typically not toxic. Eating a large amount (not likely) may cause depression, diarrhea, abdominal pain, tremors, anorexia, salivation, and vomiting. Activated charcoal is used, and in severe cases vomiting is induced and fluid replacement as necessary.

Note: This Christmas flower, introduced in the eighteenth century, looks like *Hippeastrum,* which originates from the Americas and is incorrectly sold as amaryllis. "Naked ladies" are marketed as amaryllis but are actually another species commonly known as the resurrection lily. Ingesting toxins from these plants is particularly dangerous to pets.

ANGEL'S TRUMPET

Solanaceae (*Brugmansia* sp.)

Identification: Large shrubs or small trees, with semi-woody, often many-branched, trunks. They can reach heights of 36', but typically are smaller. The leaves are alternate along the stems, generally large to 12" long and 7" across. Margin is entire or coarsely toothed and often covered with fine hairs. Distinctive large, pendulous, trumpet-shaped flowers, 6"–20" long and 4"–14" across at the corolla; colored in shades of white, yellow, pink, orange, green, or red, with a strong, pleasing fragrance, unlike other plants from Solonaceae.

Habitat: Tropical, subtropical (Ecuador, Columbia, Venezuela, Chile, Brazil).

Toxins: Seeds and leaves are especially dangerous, containing alkaloids (scopolamine, hyoscyamine, atropine, and other tropane alkaloids).

Symptoms: Psychoactive and hallucinogenic, ingestion can include paralysis of smooth muscles, confusion, tachycardia, dry mouth, diarrhea, migraine headaches, visual and auditory hallucinations, mydriasis.

First Aid: Severe intoxication is a medical emergency; evacuate to professional medical care immediately. A physician may administer an intravenous (IV) solution of physostigmine. If cholinergic effect persists, a second IV may be necessary.

Note: This is a common decorative plant, large in size, found around inns, hotels, and homes in Florida, California, Texas, and Mexico. South American indigenous cultures prepare and use it as a ritualistic hallucinogen to reach and communicate with spirits of dead ancestors.

ANGEL'S WINGS, ELEPHANT EARS, HEART OF JESUS

Araceae (*Caladium* × *hortulanum*)

Identification: Arrowhead-shaped leaves marked in varying patterns in white, pink, and red, resembling unrelated coleus; however, coleus is not toxic to humans. Plant grows to 2' in height.

Habitat: Forests and river banks of South and Central America.

Toxins: All parts have calcium oxalate.

Symptoms: Ingestion can cause severe irritation to the mouth and throat and may also be an irritant to the intestinal tract. Children as well as family pets that nibble on the foliage are at risk.

First Aid: If swallowed, call a physician. Skin treatment (irritant) requires copious water irrigation, although the irritant is more soluble in vinegar. For oral exposures, physically remove any plant material from the mouth. Check if airway is compromised; if not, ingest cold liquids, ice cream, Popsicles, or crushed ice for relief. A physician may administer via the mouth diphenhydramine elixir, providing local anesthetic and antihistaminic effects. A compromised airway treatment requires antihistamines, hospitalization, and observation until the edema improves.

CALLA LILY, CALLA
Araceae (*Zantadeschia aethiopica*)

Identification: Typically a shade-loving plant with large arrow-shaped leaves, green or green mottled with white. Snowy, showy flowers are a spathe that makes them look lily-like. Flowers are white or green with other species and cultivars of other colors.

Habitat: A common garden ornamental preferring shady, moist areas; various species subtropical to temperate— houseplant in the North, outside in the South.

Toxins: Calcium oxalate raphides.

Symptoms: Intense burning or sharp pricking of tongue and lips. Inflammation may develop if swallowed.

First Aid: Self-limiting. Drink copious amounts of cold water, or hold cold liquids in the mouth. Take demulcents for stomach, such as Mylanta, for internal exposure. If a large amount has been ingested, seek emergency medical attention.

Note: Tough, attractive plant to grow indoors—it will take abuse and keep coming at you.

BOXWOOD, BUXUS
Buxaceae (*Buxus* spp.)

Identification: Large, slow-growing, cultivated evergreen or small tree with multiple stems, used for hedge rows, borders, and topiary figures.

Habitat: In the wild, found in Macedonia, a mountain-loving shrub.

Toxins: Steroidal alkaloids including buxine make bark, leaves, roots, and twigs of *Buxus* shrubs poisonous when ingested and, to a lesser extent, cause contact dermatitis from skin contact with leaf sap. Drying the leaves does not degrade the toxin.

Symptoms: Boxwood has low toxicity to humans; reports of human poisoning are rare. Eating boxwood can cause gastrointestinal symptoms, including diarrhea, stomach pains, and vomiting; larger doses may cause respiratory problems. Skin irritation is usually mild and quickly passes. Because boxwoods, used in formal landscaping, require frequent pruning, these are shrubs that particularly sensitive individuals should avoid planting.

First Aid: Infrequent intoxication due to foul taste and copious amount needed to poison an adult. No reported human fatalities.

Note: A classic acid-soil-loving hedge, boxwood comes in over 150 varieties. What's more, deer won't eat it.

CHRYSANTHEMUM, MUMS

Asteraceae (*Chrysanthemum* spp.)

Identification: Ornamental and showy flower with numerous rays in many vibrant colors. Leave are alternate and toothed, although occasionally glabrous. In competitive exhibition flowers are classified and identified as irregular incurve, reflex, regular incurve, decorative, pompon, single, semi-double, and so on.

Habitat: Originally China, then Japan, reaching Europe as an ornamental in the seventeenth century and subsequently the Americas.

Toxins: Leaves and stalks contain arteglasin A and pyrethrins.

Symptoms: Some people develop contact dermatitis after extended exposure to garden chrysanthemums.

First Aid: Self-limiting; severe intoxication is rare.

Note: Pyrethrins are insecticidal and extracted from the seed cases of chrysanthemums. They are harmful to fish but far less dangerous to mammals and birds than most synthetic insecticides. Pyrethrins are biodegradable in the environment. Mums are an indoor purifying plant.

CROCUS, AUTUMN CROCUS

Liliaceae (*Cochicine autumnale*)

Identification: Lily with underground bulb giving rise in the autumn (sans leaves) to a flower stalk with long tubular purple and white flowers. In the spring, blade- or strap-like leaves appear and disappear before blooming.

Habitat: No longer found in the wild; intensely cultivated as house-, garden, and landscaping plants.

Toxins: Entire plant has toxin colchicine and other tropolone alkaloids. Taste is extremely bitter. Tuber occasionally confused with onions, with dangerous consequences.

Symptoms: With ingestion, burning pain in mouth and throat followed by thirst, and abdominal pain with nausea and vomiting, severe diarrhea, and loss of fluids.

First Aid: Poisoning symptoms follow a lengthy course as colchicine excretes from the body. Analgesic and atropine as well as fluid replacement are indicated with severe intoxication (atropine to relieve pain and diarrhea).

Spring crocus

Note: Crocus traditionally used to treat gout (colchicine drug from crocus). Research suggests that semen from father having used colchicine may cause birth defects.

DAFFODIL, JONQUIL
Amaryllidaceae (*Narcissus* species)

Identification: Grows from bulb; lance-shaped leaves arise at ground level from bulb; flower stalk with one or more flowers, having a flat corolla with a trumpet that flares out from the middle of the corolla. Trumpet may be large or small depending on the variety.

Habitat: Perennial native to Europe and North Africa, tolerates temperate climate.

Toxins: Bulbs, often mistaken as onions, contain lycorine family of alkaloids.

Symptoms: Nausea, vomiting, and diarrhea.

First Aid: Typically no systemic poisoning. Rehydrate.

Note: Here are a few lines of William Wordsworth's poem "I Wandered Lonely as a Cloud":

. . . For oft, when on my couch I lie
In vacant or in pensive mood,
They flash upon that inward eye
Which is the bliss of solitude;
And then my heart with pleasure fills,
And dances with the daffodils . . .

DUMB CANE, GIANT DUMB CANE, SPOTTED DUMB CANE, LEOPARD LILY

Araceae *(Dieffenbachia* species)

Identification: Tall, erect plant, unbranched, with long, large leaves splotched with ivory markings.

Habitat: Tropical and subtropical; cultivated in Hawaii and Florida, sold everywhere.

Toxins: All parts contain calcium oxalate.

Symptoms: Painful swelling of the mouth and throat occurs after ingesting dumb cane; may result in speech impediment that can last for several days. Eye contact with the juices causes pain and swelling.

First Aid: Check airway; if not compromised, ingest cold liquids, ice cream, Popsicles, or crushed ice, or take analgesics for relief. A physician may administer via mouth diphenhydramine elixir, providing local anesthetic and antihistaminic effects. Rinse eyes with copious amount of water. Compromised airway treatment requires antihistamines, hospitalization, and observation until the edema improves. Skin contact with oxalates requires copious water irrigation, although the irritant is more soluble in vinegar. For oral exposures, physically remove any plant material from the mouth; typically there may be oral edema. A physician may recommend digestive-system-soothing preparations such as Mylanta. With a large dose or allergic reaction, evacuate to emergency room for medical help. Stomach may be emptied. Administered medications may also include epinephrine or famotidine. Treatment is for anaphylactic reaction. (My poisoning with calcium oxalate was painful, causing severe stress and increased heart rate—much like a panic attack.)

Note: This plant is useful for cleaning indoor air of toxins.

ENGLISH IVY
Araliaceae (*Hedera helix*)

Identification: Aggressive, spreading, tree-climbing vine with 5-lobed leaves in juvenile shoots and stems; unlobed in mature vines.

Habitat: *Hedera helix* originated in Europe and is widely cultivated as a ground cover.

Toxins: Leaves contain didehydrofalcarinol, falcarinol, and hederasaponins, causing poisoning in cattle, dogs, sheep, and humans.

Symptoms: Difficulty breathing, convulsions, vomiting, paralysis, and coma. Dermatitis is rare but can be severe with weeping blisters that respond slowly to treatment. Berries, however, are bitter, so it is unlikely children will consume them in large quantities.

First Aid: Conservative therapy. Replace fluids.

Note: English ivy is extremely invasive and considered noxious in parts of the world where it has escaped into the wild, becoming so dense as to exclude other native species. Ivy-covered trees topple under the weight of the plant.

HOLLY BERRIES, YAUPON, AMERICAN HOLLY, ENGLISH HOLLY
Aquifoliaceae (*Ilex* spp.)

Identification: Evergreen trees and shrubs with leathery leaves. Yaupon (*Ilex vomitoria*) has yellow fruit, whereas English holly (*I. aquifolium*) and American holly (*I. opaca*) have red berries.

Habitat: American holly found in eastern United States north to Massachusetts, south to Florida, and west to Missouri and Texas. English holly is cultivated typically in the South. Yaupon typically an East Coast native found in gardens in Texas and elsewhere.

Ilex opaca

Toxins: The fruit has toxic saponins (phytosterols).

Symptoms: Nausea, vomiting, diarrhea.

First Aid: Self-limiting. Administer fluids.

Note: An important landscape decoration; hardy.

HYACINTH

Asparagaceae (*Hyacinth orientalis*)

Identification: Early spring bloomer, 4–6 linear leaves and 1–3 spikes (racemes) of flowers—excellent fragrance.

Habitat: Native to Turkey, Turkmenistan, and Israel. Cultivated perennial has escaped cultivation.

Toxins: Bulbs contain oxalic acid. Handling bulbs may cause skin irritation; wear protective gloves when handling.

Symptoms: Burning sensation in mouth if ingested; later, diarrhea and tachycardia if the victim has a panic attack (my personal experience).

First Aid: Demulcents and over-the-counter products such as Mylanta are typical with small ingestions. Replace fluids. With skin irritation, irrigate with tepid water. With a large dose or allergic reaction, evacuate to emergency room for medical help. Stomach may be emptied. Administered medications may include diphenhydramine, epinephrine, or famotidine. Treatment is for anaphylactic reaction.

Note: After flowering in spring, cut back hyacinths' flower stalks but allow the leaves to die back naturally. Water your hyacinths during dry spells in the fall. Annual application of compost should provide adequate nutrients. Flower size declines in subsequent years, so plant fresh bulbs every 2 years. (This is standard practice with all bulb plants: tulips, crocus, daffodils, and gladiolas.)

HYDRANGEA

Saxifragaceae (*Hydrangea macrophylla*)

Identification: Bush up to 15′. *H. macrophylla* flowers are blue, red, pink, or purple, color depending on the pH of the soil; that is, acidic soils (low pH) produce blue flowers, neutral soils produce pale cream flowers, and alkaline soils (high pH) result in pink or purple. This natural phenomenon is typical with numerous flowering plants.

Habitat: Native to southeastern United States and subtropical and tropical Americas.

Cultivatar hydrangea

Toxins: Leaves and buds may contain the toxic cyanogenic glycoside hydragin. Documented human poisonings typically from ingesting flower buds.

Symptoms: Sufficient ingestion induces cyanide poisoning: vomiting, abdominal pain, diarrhea, labored breathing, lethargy, and coma. Sensitive individuals may develop contact dermatitis from handling the plants.

First Aid: Gastric lavage. Activated charcoal slurry releases cyanide as it passes through the bowel, whereas a 25 percent solution of sodium thiosulfate (amount based on patient's weight) may be more effective after lavage. Severe intoxication is a medical emergency; treat acidosis, apply oxygen, and apply a cyanide antidote.

LILY OF THE VALLEY
Liliaceae (*Convallaria majalis*)

Identification: Small perennial with small bell-shaped white flowers. Plant has pairs of oblong leaves and red, fleshy berries. Plants spread into colonies by adventitious underground root system, forming dense beds.

Habitat: Eurasian but has escaped cultivation; found throughout the North Temperate Zone—a cold-climate, shade-loving plant.

Toxins: Irritating saponins and cardiac glycosides.

Symptoms: Nausea, vomiting, cramping, diarrhea, oral pain with sinus bradycardia (i.e., heart rate lowered to 50–60 beats, which may cause cardiac arrest because of insufficient oxygen to the heart).

First Aid: Moderate and extreme intoxications are a medical emergency; evacuate. Provide gastric lavage or induce vomiting, and administer activated charcoal as necessary.

Note: St. Leonard of Sussex fought against a great dragon in the woods near Horsham, England. After mortal combat lasting several hours, the saint received grievous wounds, and wherever his blood fell, lilies of the valley sprang up in the woods. The forest, which is thickly carpeted with lily of the valley, bears the name of St. Leonard's to this day.

MISTLETOE, INJERTO
Viscaceae (*Phoradendron serotinum, P. tomentosum, P. villosum; Viscum spp.*)

Identification: There are over 200 genera worldwide in this family. *P. serotinum* is a parasitic epiphyte with thick, succulent ovate leaves, margins entire (not toothed). It grows in many branched clusters typically 2 to 3 feet in diameter clinging to the limbs of host trees, producing white fruit (translucent berry).

Habitat: P. Serotinum and *P. tomentosum* found growing in the wild on mesquite trees, live oaks, and other deciduous trees from Florida north to New Jersey and then west to Texas. Drought tolerant, southern and southwestern plants.

Toxins: Phoratoxin in berries and leaves; a toxic lectin in leaves, stems, and berries.

Symptoms: Blurred vision, abdominal pain, nausea, diarrhea, blood pressure changes (hypertensive); with a (rare) significant dose, collapse and death. *Viscum* spp. contains the alkaloid tyramine with similar toxicity and symptoms. The toxin is documented as a potential abortifacient—a dangerous abortion-inducing agent; women have perished using it to induce abortions.

First Aid: Toxic lectin inhibits protein synthesis in intestinal wall. Although fatal poisonings are rare, any ingestion may lead to vomiting, cramping, and diarrhea. Medical professional (or you, if no alternative medical help is available) will administer fluids and electrolytes (Gatorade for example).

Note: Extract is potentially antidiabetic showing in vivo effect lowering blood sugar levels. *Viscum album,* a European strain, is used to treat rheumatism and as adjuvant therapy for cancerous tumor treatment; whole, cut, and powdered herb is used. The tea from *V. album* is hypotensive and may be effective against asthma, diarrhea, tachycardia, nervousness (nervine); tea traditionally used to treat amenorrhea, whooping cough, and epilepsy. Seek consultation with your holistic health-care physician, as this is a potentially dangerous drug.

OLEANDER
Apocynaceae (*Nerium oleander*)

Identification: Shrub growing to 20' with long, narrow leaves (typically 3) up to 10" long. White, red, or pink flowers in clusters, with winged and fluffy seeds born in narrow capsules ⅜" in diameter and up to 5" long.

Habitat: Mediterranean area; widespread as a garden ornamental in the United States.

Toxins: Whole plant contains cardiac glycosides.

Symptoms: Nausea, vomiting, cramping, diarrhea, oral pain with sinus bradycardia (i.e., heart rate lowered to 50–60 beats per minute, which may cause cardiac arrest because of insufficient oxygen to the heart).

First Aid: Moderate to extreme intoxication is a medical emergency; evacuate. Provide gastric lavage or induce vomiting, and administer activated charcoal as necessary.

Note: Nerium cardiac glycosides have been traditionally used to treat congestive heart failure in China. They are dose dependent and used as anti-arrhythmic agents to treat atrial fibrillation. Recent research shows small quantities of these glycosides stimulate the immune system in cancer patients.

PEONY, PAEONIA
Paeoniaceae (*Paeonia* spp.)

Identification: Herbaceous garden plant from 1.5'–5' tall; a few varieties resemble trees to 10'. Leaves are compound and lobed (deeply cut) with large, showy, and fragrant ornamental flowers, ranging the entire spectrum of colors. Flowers bloom in spring through early summer depending on latitude.

Toxic: Paeonol, concentrated in bark skin and not typically eaten; low toxicity primarily to cats and dogs. Humans have been poisoned (little documentation).

Symptoms: Diarrhea, depression, vomiting. Large ingestion required.

First Aid: Avoid plant. Condition is self-limiting.

Note: Lovely perennial garden ornamental. Often requires support because of the large size of the flowers.

STAR OF BETHELEHEM
Asparagaceae (*Ornithogalim spp.*)

Identification: Perennial growing from a bulb with thin linear basal leaves and a slender stalk, up to 12" tall, bearing clusters of typically white star-shaped flowers, often striped green.

Habitat: Native to southern Europe, southern Africa, and Caucasus; grows in temperate climates as far north as southern Michigan. Prefers sun, spreads rapidly, and is invasive.

Toxins: Toxic alkaloids, cardenolides, and bufadienolides (cardiac glycoside toxins) that interfere with electrolyte balance in the heart.

Symptoms: In humans and pets, nausea, drooling, abnormal heart rate, vomiting, dilated pupils, electrolyte abnormalities (too much potassium), weakness, collapse, tremors, seizure, and death.

First Aid: Potentially life-threatening medical emergency; evacuate to emergency medical supervision.

Note: These toxins are also in dogbane, foxglove, giant milkweed, kalanchoe, lily of the valley, and oleander. Digitalis or digoxin, a common heart medication, is used in both human and veterinary medicine. The level of poisoning varies with the particular plant, the part of the plant, and the amount consumed. All parts of the plant are generally considered toxic— even the water in the vase.

SWISS CHEESE PLANT, SPLIT-LEAF PHILODENDRON, CERIMAN
Araceae (*Monstera deliciosa*)

Identification: Woody stemmed climber with thick leaves, notched and with irregularly placed holes.

Habitat: Native to Mexico.

Toxins: Calcium oxalate. The immature fruit is very high in oxalic acid and is quite dangerous to eat.

Symptoms: General symptoms of poisoning are immediate and painful with aphonia (loss of voice), blistering, hoarseness, irritation of the mouth. Urticaria (an allergic disorder characterized by raised (swollen) patches of skin accompanied by

intense itching) can occur in sensitive individuals who ingest the ripened fruit.

First Aid: For oxalate poisoning symptoms, check if airway is compromised; if not, ingest cold liquids, ice cream, Popsicles, or crushed ice for relief. Take analgesics if necessary. A physician may administer via mouth diphenhydramine elixir, providing local anesthetic and antihistaminic effects. Rinse eyes with copious amount of water. Compromised airway treatment requires antihistamines, hospitalization, and observation until the edema improves. Skin contact with oxalates requires copious water irrigation, although the irritant is more soluble in vinegar. For oral exposures, physically remove any plant material from the mouth. With oral edema and gastrointestinal involvement, a physician may recommend digestive-system-soothing preparations such as Mylanta. For large dose or allergic reaction, a physician may empty stomach. With stomach and intestinal involvement, drink copious amounts of water. Administered medications may include diphenhydramine, epinephrine, or famotidine. Treatment is for anaphylactic reaction; my poisoning with calcium oxalate was painful, causing severe stress and increased heart rate—much like a panic attack.

RHODODENDRONS AND AZALEAS

Ericaceae (*Rhododendron* spp.)

Identification: Rhododendrons produce flowers in clusters with more than 1 flower to a stem; azaleas are a dwarf type of rhododendron with 1 flower per stem. Both genera shade tolerant. Rhododendron leathery leaves are spirally arranged, evergreen or deciduous. In some species undersides of leaves are covered with scales or hairs. Native azaleas have deciduous leaves and are shade tolerant with large leathery leaves and as mentioned a single flower per stem—indicative.

Habitat: Worldwide ornamental cultivation, varieties grow from sea level to high alpine arenas. Particularly esteemed and widespread in China, Korea, and Japan.

Toxins: A low toxicity plant, all parts contain andromedotoxins (grayanotoxins), but it is best to treat all rhododendrons as poisonous and keep them out of reach of children and pets.

Symptoms: Upset stomach and vomiting occur several hours after consumption of a toxic dose of foliage, berries, or flowers, with the victim experiencing reduced blood pressure and nausea. Loss of coordination and weakness in the muscles also presents.

First Aid: The human digestive system can break down andromedotoxins into harmless compounds, but too much consumption overwhelms the system. If above symptoms present, evacuate to professional medical help.

Note: Honey produced by bees from the flowers and the nectar may be toxic (honey intoxification). Bees are often poisoned. Honey intoxification, understood for 2,500 years, presents in animals; they suffer the same symptoms as above and may be more susceptible.

TULIPS

Liliaceae (*Tulipa* spp.)

Identification: Spring-blooming perennials from bulbs with whorl of 4"–28" bladelike leaves. Large flower blooming on end of thick hollow stem, 1 flower per stem; however, a few cultivars produce more than 1 flower per stem. Sepals and petals (3 each) in a wide variety of colors and shapes. Fruit is a leathery capsule with numerous flat, disk-shaped seeds.

Habitat: Cultivated worldwide. Wild types found in Southern Europe, Pakistan, northwestern China, North Africa, Palestine, Turkey, Israel.

Toxins: Toxic lactones and antimicrobial tuliposides in bulb.

Symptoms: Typical signs include profuse drooling, vomiting, or even diarrhea, tachycardia, difficulty breathing.

First Aid: If symptoms present, evacuate to emergency medical care.

Note: Flower petals are edible; see *Edible Flowers* DVD available from herbvideos.com.

FRUIT TREE TOXINS

Several fruit trees bear fruit with potentially toxic seeds. The fruits themselves are harmless and nutritious, but seeds from apples, black cherries, choke cherries, peaches, pears, and apricots contain amygdalin that is metabolized as hydrogen cyanide, which is toxic and can make you ill—and given a large enough dose, it can cause death. The seeds from cherries and apples aren't a huge concern since it would take a very large quantity to induce toxicity. However, peach and apricot seeds are a bigger problem. Avoid eating these seeds!

Hydrogen cyanide impedes blood from carrying oxygen. A fatal dose of cyanide can be as little as 1.5 mg/kg of body weight. An apricot kernel contains up to 0.5 mg of cyanide, thus consuming 150 seeds could be lethal. Albeit this is an unlikely scenario, one fatality in the United States has been reported. I am compelled to mention it, as bags of apricot kernels, which can be eaten as an alternative cancer treatment, are available for purchase online and in health food stores. Sweet kernels of cultivars contain less amygdalin and consequently less cyanide than the bitter kernels of apricots.

YEW, ENGLISH YEW, PACIFIC YEW

Taxaceae (*Taxus baccata*, *Taxus brevifolia*)

Identification: English yew is a large shrub or small tree, evergreen, with branches alternate and reddish-brown scaled bark (thinly scaled). Needles to 1" in length grow in opposite pairs along the twigs. Hard seeds show in red cup of fruit.

Pacific yew, Taxus brevifolia

Habitat: Tolerates shade. Popular ornamental found nationwide and native to Europe and North Africa.

Toxins: Taxol, a taxine alkaloid.

Symptoms: Dizziness, dry mouth, abdominal cramps, vomiting. Face is pale, lips blue (cyanotic). Weakness leads to coma, and respiratory and cardiac failure.

First Aid: Simply chewing the leaves may initiate severe allergic reaction. Ingestion is a medical emergency! Evacuate stomach and administer slurry of activated charcoal. Electrocardiogram administered; in severe cases, a pacemaker applied.

Note: Taxol and its manufactured derivatives tie up mitotic spindles so cells cannot divide. Taxol is the model of a patented and frequently used cancer therapy drug. In the 1990s *T. brevifolia* was grown or gathered from the wild, initially in large volume, to isolate the drug. Once isolated, researchers modeled taxol into a synthetic and made it available in relative abundance for therapeutic research.

Chapter Six

Psychoactive Plants

In this chapter, we enter the realm of plants producing psychoactive chemistry. Throughout history, and certainly prehistory, humans have used plant preparations to induce spiritual connections, hallucinations, euphoria, peak performance, and stupor. Humans from all continents pursue and use plant drugs, regardless of negative consequences. Whether it be alcohol, tobacco, caffeine, cocaine, marijuana, or heroin (and the list goes on and on), most people use drugs, and most people avoid addiction, but too many do not. Science suggests a compromised prefrontal cortical function and consequential loss of inhibitory control push many to naturally calm and soothe themselves—to self-medicate, if you will. The powerful mood-regulating capacity of plant drugs, as I have often said, "takes the pressure off living." But to succumb to the sirens of psychoactive plant chemistry is too often a failure and tragedy. Research suggests deficiencies in the brain's reward system are to blame. Strong positive reinforcement of many phytochemical highs draw the abuser back for more. Pleasure seeking, relaxation, stimulation, narcissism, feelings of inadequacy, anger, genetic predisposition, and compulsive behavior lure healthy individuals into the use, misuse, and addictive syndrome. They feel empowered—stoked with self-confidence and revelation.

The story begins with alcohol. Alcohols are naturally occurring compounds in plants. The small amounts of alcohol from plant metabolism have little effect on us, but when we take plant parts—flowers, leaves, seeds, roots, fruits, and water—and ferment them in the presence of yeast, we can concentrate alcohol as a metabolic by-product. Of all the drugs emanating from plants, alcohol is the most widely used—and for too many, the most debilitating. Intoxicated people cause an inordinate amount of fatal traffic accidents, hand-gun deaths, robberies, and other illegal actions.

ALCOHOL

Identification: Beer, wine, schnapps, vodka, gin, rum, bourbon, mezcal, pulque . . .

Habitat: From plant parts available worldwide.

Toxins/Drugs: Alcohol (ethanol: CH_3CH_2OH), a solvent with low lipid solubility and completely miscible (homogeneous mix) in water, is fermented from carbohydrates by airborne yeast where the microbe converts sugar into carbon dioxide and alcohol. Alcohol's short

Americans consume over 850 million gallons of wine per year.

metabolic pathway (stomach and small intestine) provides the fastest source of calories from food. In contrast to other drugs discussed here, it takes a relatively large amount of alcohol to get the desired effect. Low lipid (fat) solubility of alcohol and high diffusion rate shortens the duration of effects; that is, alcohol does not bind to fats as do longer-acting drugs like Valium (diazepam). So alcohol enters the highly vascular, blood-rich brain quickly—and the effects are quickly felt, and soon enough dispersed.

Symptoms: Symptoms of overdose include confusion, stupor, vomiting, seizures, slow and irregular breathing. Victim presents blue-tinged skin or pale skin with low body temperature (hypothermia). If unconscious—that is, if the victim cannot be roused—the person is at risk of dying. Ethyl alcohol (or ethanol) is a central nervous system stimulant in low doses; in moderate doses, it's a central nervous system depressant. Lower doses stimulate locomotor activity. When alcohol consumption is limited to an ounce or two, this central nervous system effect quickly dissimilates. The rate of absorption of alcohol into the blood is fastest when ingested as a 15 to 30 percent solution (common in wine). In concentrations above this level, alcohol depresses peristalsis (wavelike smooth muscle contraction to move food through the digestive tract) and may produce a pyloric valve spasm between the stomach and duodenum (entrance to the small intestine). This slows the assimilation of alcohol in the small intestine (an effect that also can lead to cramps and constipation). About 90 percent of alcohol is absorbed from the small intestine and only 10 percent from the stomach. Food, especially protein and carbohydrates, slow the absorption of alcohol in the stomach. Other classic symptoms of intoxification are relaxation, increased appetite, mood elevation, reduced inhibition, reduced reaction time, slurred speech, and impaired motor skills. The drug is also a powerful diuretic, astringent, and analgesic.

First Aid: If someone has alcohol poisoning, seek immediate medical care. In an emergency (if person is unconscious and breathing less than eight times a minute, or has repeated, uncontrolled vomiting) call 911 or your local emergency number immediately. Never assume that a person will "sleep off" alcohol poisoning. Be sure to tell hospital emergency personnel the kind and amount of alcohol the person drank, and when.

Note: Alcohol was probably one of the first plant-based drugs abused by prehistoric man. It is an anodyne that relaxes, calms, soothes, and comforts. It has an initial euphoric effect and reduces anxiety. These factors account for its desirability and universal use.

Accidental fermentation of fruit juices, honey, potato starch, and grain beverages in prehistoric times gave rise to today's broad use of alcoholic beverages worldwide. Perhaps the oldest alcoholic beverage is mead, a Paleolithic fermentation produced from honey and water. Egyptians brewed and fermented wine and beer over 5,700 years ago. The Islamic culture stands out for its staunch alcohol temperance, but by AD 800, Arabs learned how to concentrate alcohol through distillation. The word *alcohol* is Arabic (*alkuhl*) meaning "something subtle." At near-lethal dose alcohol is a general anesthetic and was used as such during nineteenth-century surgery.

As an anesthetic, the duration of alcohol is short lived. This required a swift and deft knife wielded by battle surgeons, and too often their swiftness led to irrecoverable mistakes: wrong limbs amputated, organs incised and destroyed leading to sepsis, putrefaction, and death. A Russian physician once explained to me how in the old Soviet Union alcohol and lily of the valley (*Convallaria majalis*) were used together to treat dropsy. The practitioner administered alcohol intravenously as a diuretic and analgesic, while lily of the valley was dosed orally both for its stimulating effect on left ventricle contraction, and its capacity to dilate coronary arteries.

Chronic, high alcohol consumption increases cancer-inducing homocysteine levels in the blood.

Alcohol and pregnancy don't mix! Alcohol readily passes into fetal circulation, subjecting the fetus to the effects of the drug. This may lead to fetal alcohol syndrome, causing abnormal changes in the infant's brain and leading to physical and mental handicaps. Some research suggests prenatal consumption of alcohol by a mother may induce attention deficit hyperactivity disorder (ADHD) in children.

AYAHAUSCA, *YAGE, CAAPI,* SOUL VINE
Malpighiaceae (*Banisteriopsis caapi*)
Identification: A shrub or climbing, twisting vine (or liana) with chocolate brown, smooth bark. Leaves are opposite, 6"–7" long, 3" wide, oval, double tapered, margins entire. Flowers are pink with 10 stamens. Fruit is a small nut. Seeds are fan-shaped; green when fresh, and brown when mature.

Habitat: Tropical, Peru and other Amazonian regions.

Toxins/Drugs: Beta-arboline alkaloids and monoamine oxidase (MAOI) inhibitors: harmine, harmaline—a subtle psychedelic, slightly hallucinogenic alkaloid.

Symptoms: Psychedelic sensory enhancements, slightly hallucinogenic, but primarily a calming, "soul cleansing" drug. An ayahuasca preparation that is smoked may cause a feeling of heaviness, lethargy, dizziness, trembling, and nausea. It is a sialagogue (increases salivation). The high occurs about 5–10 minutes after smoking, with various amounts of sensory enhancement.

First Aid: Because the drug has MAO inhibitors (MAOI), care must be taken with users who are on medicines that restrict the use of MAOI. In addition, MAO inactivates neurotransmitters, thus too much or too little is a problem. Low or high levels of MAO are associated with specific psychiatric disorders such as depression, schizophrenia, and attention deficit disorder. Irregular amounts of MAO leave a person susceptible to substance abuse. Because MAO levels affect epinephrine, dopamine, and norepinephrine levels, harmaline, a reversible monoamine inhibitor, can lead to extreme hypertension crisis, serotonin poisoning, and possibly death. Victim must discontinue use of drug, and in extreme cases, a serotonin antagonist is administered. Emotional support is helpful to control excessive agitation (which may require a sedative).

Note: According to Amazonian natives, the drug is a spiritual purgative, cleansing the body and opening the mind.

BETEL NUT, ARECA PALM, ARECA NUT, BETEL PALM

Arecaceae (*Areca catechu*)

Identification: Betel nut is the seed of the areca palm (areca nut), a medium-size palm to 65' tall and up to 9" thick. Leaves are pinnate with crowded palm leaflets about 7' long, more or less. Male and female flowers are creamy white, scented; male flowers smaller. Palm produces up to 18 pounds of nuts per tree per year. Nut is a reddish ovoid or elliptical drupe, somewhat flattened.

Habitat: Tropical wet climates of East Africa, Southeast Asia, India, Polynesia; available at eastern groceries in the United States.

Toxins/Drugs: Contains stimulant arecoline and volatile oils (chavibetol, eugenol, anethole, chamicol, safrole). Areca nut is typically chewed with betel leaves of the Piperaceae family and lime therefore the combination is commonly called betel nut.

Symptoms: Mild stimulant and analgesic used like coffee for its caffeine-like effect. Nut chewed with mineral lime and betel leaf discolors teeth and makes user prone to gum disease and tooth loss. It is carcinogenic and linked to oral cancers—habitual users are almost ten times more likely to get these cancers than the nonuser. Teratogenic effects (congenital abnormalities) possible on newborn when betel nut and betel leaves chewed by pregnant women.

First Aid: Self-limiting. Cessation of use can prevent loss of teeth, gum disease, and oral cancers.

Note: I will never forget a flight in 1966 on a DC-3 from Kathmandu to a little airfield in Nepal. The flight attendant served us a sandwich in a brown bag. Down in the bottom of the bag was half a betel nut (areca nut). I watched the other Nepalese passengers stick the nuts in their mouths, then suck and bite them. I followed the crowd. First time around this was not a pleasant experience: It was as hard as rock, tasted a bit like clove; unmemorable, I would have preferred coffee, and there was no effect I could notice. Chemistry may be prophylactic to worm infections. Leaves and nut (betel nut) also used to treat dyspepsia, coughs, bronchitis, asthma (helps cut excess mucus), arthritis, and impotency. Used traditionally as Westerners use coffee and applied medicinally to treat middle ear infections and inflammations.

COCAINE, COCA
Erythroxylacea (*Erythroxylon coca*)
Identification: Evergreen shrub grows 7'–10' tall, with straight branches. Thin leaves are oval and taper at both ends. Small flowers in clusters with short stalks; corolla is composed of 5 yellowish-white petals with heart-shaped anthers. Pistil has 3 carpels; berries red.

SHUTTERSTOCK.COM

Habitat: Andean mountain dweller (Peru, Bolivia).

Toxins/Drugs: Coca alkaloid. When chewed, coca acts as a mild stimulant and suppresses hunger, thirst, pain, and fatigue. Historical documentation suggests that raw coca is not addictive. There appear to be no deleterious effects from the consumption of the leaf in its natural form, thus leading to the logical conclusion that chewing raw coca leaf is not habit-forming, and there is no empirical evidence showing the coca plant's potential for addiction. In fact, unprocessed coca helps recovering cocaine addicts to wean off the drug in favor of traditional leaf chewing and to live their lives without preoccupying themselves with the next fix.

Symptoms: This psycho-stimulating alkaloid inhibits uptake of norepinephrine and dopamine, providing a euphoric, hallucinogenic, anesthetic, antibacterial, and ergogenic (increasing work output) effect. Snorting the drug may cause a loss of smell, nosebleeds, hoarseness, swallowing difficulty, and runny nose, whereas snorting rock crystal crack escalates symptoms of irritability, anxiety, paranoia, and restlessness.

Addictive, chronic use of cocaine often leads to heart attacks, respiratory failure, stroke, digestive disorders, allergic reactions, skin infections, mouth sores, stomach ulcers, destructive loss of blood flow to the bowels, and even death—not as obvious is the potential for HIV infection when sharing needles. Victims of abuse lose touch with reality, suffer from severe paranoia (a temporary state of paranoid psychosis), and experience auditory hallucinations. Cocaine passes through the placenta and impairs fetal development. Negative results lead to preterm births, low birth weight, and more frequent instances of sudden infant death syndrome (SIDS). Cognitive

development is impaired and addiction with withdrawal symptoms exhibited.
First Aid: Various forms of treatment include psychotherapy, acupuncture, prize reinforcement (i.e., patient given money for staying clean), peer reinforcement, and spiritual enhancement (much like Alcoholics Anonymous). Research shows that clinically induced viral bacteriophages in laboratory models may eliminate the load of cocaine in the brain, thereby reducing dependency.

Note: Cocaine extracted from the coca leaf is pounded into a paste, and the paste converted to cocaine hydrochloride salt—the water-soluble crystalline form is snorted or mixed in drinks. Snorting is as potent as inhaling or injecting the drug. Cocaine hydrochloride, however, is heat degradable and worthless as a "smoke." But capable chemists percolate the hydrochloride out of the cocaine with an alkaline solution, producing freebase, crack, or rock cocaine—a highly addictive substance that can be smoked, heightening the pharmacological effects of the drug. Intravenous injection or freebasing is the most potent abuse of cocaine. On the other hand, leaf chewing is not as intense and euphoric as the purified forms of cocaine—and once again leaf chewing is not addictive.

Indigenous people of the eastern Andes have used coca leaves for over 5,000 years. Incas used the drug in rituals and ceremonies revering the sun god. Leaves chewed with a bit of lime or ash raises the pH and improves absorption of the active principle through the mucous membranes of the oral cavity. Spanish conquistadores outlawed the use of cocaine briefly but gave it another try when they discovered their Inca slaves worked harder and longer while on the drug. Sigmund Freud used cocaine to treat morphine addiction. Freud also recommended its use for treating alcoholism and depression. Pharmacist John Pemberton invented Coca-Cola, a "soft drink" made with cocaine and caffeine in response to coke's widespread use in Vin Mariani, a concoction of wine and cocaine—what was considered a nineteenth-century cure-all. Parke, Davis & Company offered cocaine inhalants and cocaine-laced cigars and cigarettes. Soon there were other Coke knockoffs: Nerv Ola, and Koca Nola. Prior to 1914, dentists gave painkilling cocaine tooth drops to babies cutting teeth. In 1910, President Taft labeled cocaine "public enemy number one." Laws passed at the local and national level banned cocaine use (including the 1914 Harrison Narcotics Tax Act). Prohibition of alcohol in 1920 boosted the illicit sales of cocaine products. Abuse was widespread. Use of the drug went underground. Drug experimentation in the 1960s spawned a wave of increased use. According to the 2012 National Survey of Drug Use and Health approximately 1.6 million people 12 years of age or older used cocaine in 2012.

COFFEE, JOE, JAVA
Rubiaceae (*Coffea Arabica*; *C. canephora*)
Identification: Berry-producing evergreen shrub that grows from 5' to 10' tall. Leaves are dark green, glossy, 5"–6" long and 2.5" wide. Plant produce clusters of white and fragrant flowers a bit over 0.5" in length. Two oval green beans

(seeds) inside each cherry (fruit). The beans then roast to brown or black.

Habitat: Originated at higher altitudes in Ethiopia, Sudan, and northern Kenya, and now cultivated in every hemisphere and on four continents—often grown under banana trees.

Toxins/Drugs: Caffeine is a lipid (fat) soluble compound, a methylxanthine stimulant found in coffee, tea, maté leaves, guarana paste, cola nuts, chocolate, and numerous other plant products.

Symptoms: Chronic and large-volume consumption of caffeinated beverages leads to "caffeinism." Symptoms include insomnia, restlessness, and anxiety with increased heart rate. In the extreme, a person may suffer from severe psychological disturbance (when consuming over ten cups of coffee per day or 1,000 mg of caffeine). Caffeine affects locomotor activity, anxiety, blood pressure, and respiration; it is diuretic and releases epinephrine, and may, in some cases, cause panic attacks. It mobilizes the metabolism of fatty acids, increases endurance, and increases homocysteine blood concentrations linked to dementia and cancer. Caffeine decreases blood flow to the brain and causes glycogen depletion in the liver and muscles (trial was with 330 mg caffeine 60 minutes before exercise).

First Aid: Vitamin E therapy and abstinence from caffeine has been helpful. Abstinence is curative.

Note: Caffeine is an ingredient in pharmaceutical preparations including Anacin, Excedrin, Vivarin, and No Doz. Many soft drinks promising an energy boost have caffeine as an ingredient. A few people are less sensitive to caffeine and may not be as severely affected. A person who attempts to stop drinking coffee may experience headaches, fatigue, poor concentration, and compromised motor activity. Craving for coffee may be so severe as to leave the abstainer dysfunctional.

Therapeutically caffeine acts synergistically with aspirin for treating non-migraine headaches. Cafergot is a combination of caffeine and ergotamine used for treating migraines. Newborn infants who have periodic cessation of breathing (apneic episodes) have been treated with caffeine. As a stimulant, there is the intriguing possibility that caffeine may actually calm a hyperactive child who had been taking Ritalin or Prozac. Coffee does not speed alcohol metabolism; it is not a cure for a hangover. As a stimulant, caffeine may help sprinters, but it may be detrimental for endurance or distance athletes and athletes who participate in events that go beyond a few minutes. Caffeine increases energy expenditure by stimulating the adrenal glands to release epinephrine. Naturopathic physicians suggest that long-term, frequent use of caffeine may exhaust the adrenal glands.

Caffeine products are not a good substitute for water because, as a diuretic, it actually increases excretion of liquids and salts (electrolytes) from the body.

A caffeine-imbibing child who drinks two Coca-Colas per day and weighs approximately sixty pounds receives the metabolic equivalent of eight cups of coffee, making the youngster sleepless, restless, and prone to all the physiological stressors of caffeine consumption. Pregnant mothers should curtail their caffeine consumption because there is evidence that heavy coffee drinkers may have children with lower birth weight. For nursing mothers, caffeinated coffee drinking during lactation may make the breast-fed youngster irritable and restless, perhaps unable to sleep; even one cup per day may interfere with the ability of the child to absorb and use iron. Fibrocystic breast disease may be associated with caffeine consumption. Osteoporosis may be accelerated by caffeine consumption because of the drug's ability to increase calcium excretion. Diuretic effect of caffeine increases excretion of calcium, potassium, magnesium, iron, and zinc. A research study reviewed evidence linking caffeine consumption with an increased incidence of coronary heart disease; increased blood pressure is indicative of the stress that caffeine can put on the heart.

Caffeine is completely absorbed in the digestive tract within approximately forty-five minutes. Absorption occurs in the stomach and small intestine, with the small intestine being the main site of absorption. The half-life of caffeine in a human is 2.5–4.5 hours. People who drink throughout the day may experience rising plasma concentrations of caffeine. Most clearing occurs during sleep. The liver metabolizes most of the caffeine and its metabolites that are then excreted through the urine, with about 5 percent or less through the feces.

Caffeine may improve performance in several measurable tasks. A survey in Great Britain of 7,000 men and women caffeine drinkers tested their performance of several tasks: simple reaction time, choice reaction time, incidental verbal memory, visual/spatial reasoning. Results showed an improvement in task performance significant to caffeine consumption with each task. Optimum performance for all four tasks appeared to require four cups of coffee equivalent per day. Thus, one might obtain increased performance at the cost of several physiological deficits such as increased arousal, fatigue, anxiety, increased respiration, and elevated blood pressure.

DATURA, JIMSONWEED
Solanaceae (*Datura stramonium, D. meteloides*)

Identification: Hollow upright or branched stem grows 3'–4' tall. Trumpetlike white to light violet flower is distinctive with an offensive odor (at least for this author). Seed capsule studded with spines. Leaves are long stemmed, toothed, and coarse

textured. Pungent odor increases when leaves and stems are crushed.

Habitat: Found along roadsides, disturbed ground, and in corn- and bean fields throughout the United States. *Datura meteloides* is more common in the Southwest. It is a popular, showy garden flower throughout the Midwest.

Toxins/Drugs: Belladonna alkaloids, which include scopolamine, atropine, and hyoscyamine (also called daturine).

Symptoms: Dry mouth, intoxication, dilated pupils, also reddening of face and neck, delirium, hallucinations, tachycardia, and elevated blood pressure—severe overdose with as few as 20 seeds may lead to death.

First Aid: Severe intoxication is a medical emergency; evacuate to professional medical practitioners immediately. A physician may administer an intravenous (IV) solution of physostigmine. If cholinergic (a substance that produces, alters, or releases acetylcholine) effect persists, a second IV is necessary.

Note: This is a dangerous hallucinogen abused by unaware teenagers. The potentially fatal dose varies from plant to plant. The "get high" dose of imbibed seeds is very close to the lethal dose. The name Jamestown weed has its genesis in the Revolutionary War: In Jamestown, British soldiers consumed it, believing it edible, and spent nearly a fortnight in various altered mental states—and then they lost the war!

FLY AGARIC, FLY AMANITA, PANTHER CAP
Amanitaceae (*Amanita muscaria; Amanita pantherina*)

Identification: Fly agaric is a large white-gilled mushroom emerging from white egg having a red cap with white spots or pyramid-like yellow warts. Warts are remnants of the veil that covered the mushroom at birth. When young, there is a yellowish layer of skin under the veil; then, as the fungus grows, a red color emerges through the broken veil, and warts (veil remnants) become less prominent; in fact, size of warts does not change, but they appear smaller as cap expands. Cap grows from globular to hemispherical, and finally to platelike or flat at maturity. Red cap is 3"–8" in diameter. Red color fades with age. Gills are white. Oval spores form a white print. Slightly brittle and fibrous stem or stipe is white, 2"–8" tall; cap 0.4"–0.8" wide. Basal egg or bulb bears veil remnants in 2–4 distinct rings. A wide white ring is located between egg remnants and gills. Mild odor. Panther cap is brown and mottled with warts.

Habitat: Found in temperate regions of North America, Europe, Russia, China, and the Southern Hemisphere; symbiotic with pine trees and various deciduous trees. Of interest, Alaska is considered the cradle of civilization for the plant from which its diaspora began.

Toxins/Drugs: Muscimol from ibotenic acid when the mushroom is consumed or dried.

Symptoms: This hallucinogenic intoxicant and entheogen is often used in religious, shamanic, or spiritual rituals by several cultures. It contains muscimol, a mild relaxant, which can create a range of experiences from joy to depression. People may chant, sing, dance, or become paranoid (fearful).

First Aid: Activated charcoal slurry is given, and gastric lavage applied in severe intoxication. Do not induce vomiting because of deleterious effects of regurgitating, including choking. With no antidote, supportive care is necessary. Delirious and agitated victims may be treated with verbal support, reassuring them of a positive outcome, but in severe agitation physical restraints may be used. Physicians may treat other related symptoms with therapeutics as necessary—fluid replacement recommended. As of this writing, there have been no reported deaths from the use of this mushroom as a drug or food in the twentieth and twenty-first centuries—sickness yes; death, not yet.

Note: Fly agaric is widely eaten in Europe, Asia, and North America after boiling and sautéing. Toxin is water soluble, and water partially denatures the toxin and draws it from the mushroom. For centuries, and by many cultures, the mushroom has been sprinkled in milk and used as an insecticide to kill flies; scientific speculation suggests flies seek the plant to hallucinate, attracted by an enticing (and intoxicating) chemical, 1,3-diolein. For more on *Panaeolus* spp. and *Psilocybe* mushrooms see FalconGuides' *North American Mushrooms: A Field Guide to Edible and Inedible Fungi* (Globe Pequot Press).

MARIJUANA, WEED, HEMP, GANJA, REEFER, POT, PANAMA RED

Cannabaceae (*Cannabis sativa*)

Identification: Small to large plant. Potent hybrids are smaller. Leaves are 5-bladed, serrated (toothed) leaflets. Plant has a tough fibrous stem. Green female flower buds are the sought after part.

High-potency hybrid marijuana buds

Habitat: Subtropical and temperate; wild strain is drought tolerant and will grow equally well on drained and marshy wet soils. In Michigan, before the legalization of medical marijuana in 2008, it was typically grown in canvas or coarse fiber grain sacks or flour bags stuffed with compost, and then placed atop rich wetland earth (or any other somewhat inaccessible area where plants are hidden).

Toxins/Drugs: Cannabinoids to include 1-THC and sixty-one other cannabinoids and numerous volatile oils to include humules, caryophyllene, alpha-pinenes, beta-pinenes, beta-ocimene, limonene, myrcene, and numerous flavonoids. Tetrahydrocannabinol (THC) extracted in oil is an illegal psychoactive condiment used in homemade brownie and cookie mixes to provide a "high." THC is lipophyllic, fat loving, and is contained in flower heads (female buds) and smoked or processed into concentrated doses such as blond and black hashish.

Symptoms: May cause either clear (apparent) or confused thinking (all at the same time equals the psychedelic effect). These effects, after repeated use, may lead to anxiety, paranoia, confusion, and unclear thinking, but not typically. Empathy may be affected, and disassociation manifested. In a few people effects go to a higher level; in others effects are less. Psychotropic effects include "buzz," euphoria ("stoned"), lost incentive (temporary), lost drive, diluted inhibition, and acute sensitivity to stimuli (sensory stimulant) including increased sensitivity to taste (craving), color, sound, heat, and cold. Potent dose alters spatial and time perception. Symptoms are transitory and short term (up to 6 hours). New hybrids are more intense and cultivated for particular traits: analgesic, euphoric, sedative. The effect of the drug is dependent on the individual, the environment, and the quality and quantity of drug: that is, being with friends in a natural, safe setting often leads to either a robust experience or meditative relaxation.

First Aid: Self-limiting: User may need physical help when walking. He or she may become disoriented and unable to move for a period of time, in some cases 2–3 hours. Typically they are in a very sedate condition, seemingly engrossed (trancelike) with sensory stimuli enhanced (music, nature, food, etc.). Physical and emotional support will carry the day. Keep in mind that the individual may not be able to rise for a restroom excursion.

Note: Marijuana may treat contact dermatitis, poison ivy. The Cherokee used marijuana as a stimulant, improving mental attitude in sick patients, giving them the will to go on and get well. This mild sedative appeared to help soldiers deal with the Vietnam War; Vietnam protesters used the drug for the same reason. While working with the Department of Defense in Asia and Europe the drug (typically blond and black hashish from Turkey) was readily available and openly used by officers and enlisted men. Herbal and culinary preparations of flower heads are antiemetic, antinausea, analgesic, a bronchial dilator, somewhat anti-asthmatic, and are used traditionally to treat gout, malaria, forgetfulness, beriberi, constipation, and anxiety. In Europe, it is used externally in balms and as a poultice for wounds, pain, soreness, infections. Also smoked or eaten to treat insomnia, arthritis, epilepsy, asthma, bronchitis, whooping cough, polyneuropathy. Eating the prepared drug circumvents the rasping, irritating effect of inhaling the hot smoke.

In modern medical practice, marijuana is used to treat pain and symptoms of cancer, ulcers, emphysema, bronchitis, anxiety, hysteria, neurasthenia. Marinol (dronabinol) is a commercial cannabis derivative used as an appetite stimulant for anorexia, loss of appetite due to cancer, and as an antiemetic caused by cancer treatments. Also a favored drug for AIDS patients. Chronic use may cause symptoms similar to chronic cigarette smoking such as bronchitis and laryngitis. Although marijuana research suggests that smoking the drug is less deleterious than smoking cigarettes, it is a health hazard. Like most drugs, pregnant and nursing mothers should avoid the drug.

Warning: An illegal drug in many states. Avoid use while driving or operating machinery. Studies suggest it may induce reversible impotency after long and continued use.

MESCAL BEAN, CORAL BEAN, PAGODA TREE, RED HOTS, TEXAS MOUNTAIN LAUREL
Leguminosae *(Fabaceae)*
(Sophora secundiflora* and *S. tomentosa)

Identification: Shrub to small tree, compound leaves, typically 9 leaflets, with a single leaflet at the apex of the leaf and purple flowers in colorful racemes. Seeds contained in woody pods are bright red in color. *S. tomentosa* is a shrub with compound leaves, yellow flowers in racemes with yellow seeds contained in a pealike pod.

Habitat: Both species found in southwestern United States and Baja Mexico.

Toxins/Drugs: Seeds contain cytosine and related family of toxins similar in effects and chemistry to nicotine.

Symptoms: Nausea, vomiting, headache, salivation, perspiration, diarrhea, perhaps vertigo. With serious intoxication, convulsions and paralysis of respiratory muscles possible; death rare.

First Aid: Fluid replacement in less severe cases and airway management and respiratory support in severe intoxication.

MORNING GLORY
Convolvulaceae (*Ipomoea* spp.)

Identification: Climbing vine or shrub with adventitious roots, rapidly spreading. Trumpet-shaped flower, white or blue, but many species have various hues. Flower typically opens in morning. Seed is black and contains the drug.

Habitat: Over 500 species worldwide—tolerant of both poor, dry soils and wetlands. Mexican varieties are especially hallucinogenic. *I. purpurea* ("manto de la Virgen") found in the Yucatán has been used for hundreds of years in Mayan medicine and rituals. Seeds also used by the indigenous Zapotecs from which they made the powerful drug badoh negro; morning glories of this species grow profusely on the eastern shore of Cozumel island, throughout the Yucatán, and in and around Oaxaca. Numerous members of the morning glory family inhabit the Hawaiian Islands and are used as food and medicine there, including *I. indica, I. caririca,* and *I. pes-caprae.* Years ago, I brought several wild varieties and cultivars into my garden, a nuisance that spreads vigorously everywhere.

Toxins/Drugs: Seeds contain indole alkaloids, LSA, and ergoline alkaloids: ergonovine and ergine that are psychedelic with an effect similar to LSD—but requires a large dose of seeds. Seeds found in garden centers are often coated with methylmercury, pesticides, and fungicides. These toxic substances cause neural destruction and liver damage. Never imbibe commercially purchased seeds.

Symptoms: With a sufficient dose victim may experience nausea, cramps, possibly vomiting, next-day diarrhea, hallucinations, flushing, reduced blood pressure, occasional anxiety, and eventually drowsiness.

First Aid: Low level of toxicity, but even a good trip can be a bad trip. Ingesting the powdered seeds creates nausea and possibly vomiting. Up to and over 1,000 seeds can be taken by one person with little hallucinogenic effect, but producing cramps, nausea, vomiting, and diarrhea. Effects last for up to 5–6 hours; drowsiness persists, inducing sleep and, upon wakening, perhaps an afterglow—you survived.

Note: Various species have purgative activity, roots used as a laxative to relieve constipation including *Ipomoea purga* syn. *I. jalapa.* A few species are hemostatic. Others claimed as aphrodisiacs and hallucinogens (seeds used).

NUX VOMICA, POISON NUT, QUAKER BUTTONS, STRYCHNINE

Loganaceae (*Strychnos nux vomica*)

Identification: Deciduous tree with a short, thick trunk. Irregular branches covered with smooth ash-colored bark. Young branches green and shiny. Leaves are ovate, opposite, and 2"–4" long and 2"-3" wide. Flowers are pale green and funnel shaped. Fruit is round, about the size of an apple, green to orange in color.

Habitat: Native to India, Australia, and Southeast Asia, tropical to subtropical, found in the United States growing wild and cultivated.

Toxins/Drugs: Highly poisonous alkaloids: strychnine and brucine from the seeds, flowers, and bark. *Strychnos nux vomica* reportedly has also been used as an adulterant in LSD. It is a deadly poison, but a toxic dose cannot be absorbed on a small LSD tab (blotter used to administer a dose of LSD).

Symptoms: Convulsions due to a simultaneous stimulation (auditory and visual) of the motor or sensory ganglia of the spinal cord. During the convulsions there is a rise in blood pressure. Brucine closely resembles strychnine in its action but is slightly less poisonous.

First Aid: Medical emergency—call 911. A physician will maintain an open airway and support breathing. A muscle relaxant and general anesthetic may be used to control convulsions. Renal pathway must be kept open to void toxins presented by muscle breakdown from being transported to kidneys. External cooling is required to prevent hyperthermia and intravenous sodium bicarbonate administered to correct acidosis.

Note: Drug extracted from the seeds, which are removed from the fruit when ripe and then cleaned, dried, and sorted. In clinical studies, strychnine heightens visual, auditory, and cutaneous sensitivity. In one rat study, a clap of the hands sends a strychnine-dosed rat into convulsive activity. This supersensitivity initiated by strychnine's antagonizing effect on the inhibitory neurotransmitter glycine—perhaps why in folk medicine strychnine is used as an aphrodisiac. It is a potent rat and rodent poison.

OPIUM POPPY

Papaveraceae (*Papaver somniferum*)

Identification: Single and double flowers varying in color and physical characteristics, typically blue, purple, or white flowers, to 5" wide. Plants are about 3' tall; leaves are lobed, toothed, and silver-green in color. Seed pods are large, green, and contain numerous seeds. Color of seeds and amount of seeds vary, as does drug alkaloid content. It is a perennial in climates it can tolerate; in Michigan, a severe winter will kill the roots. Lowest dose of opiates are in 'Norman' and 'Przemko' varieties. Seeds and non-narcotic oil are used in bakery products and for seasoning. *P. sominifera* seeds widely available in the United States for ornamental use; drawing the drug from the plant is illegal.

SHUTTERSTOCK.COM

Habitat: Globally a broad range. Much is grown in the Middle East, including Turkey. I have grown it in my garden. It is a beautiful garden flower.

Toxins/Drugs: Alkaloid opiates, heroin, morphine, codeine, thebaine, papaverine, narcotine, narceine.

Preparation: Crude drug prepared by cutting skin of fruit, inducing an ooze of resin. Resin collected, dried, and powdered.

Symptoms: Opiates are sedative and produce feelings of euphoria and a sense of well-being as well as a broad array of psycho and physical side effects. It is a highly addictive substance that leads to tolerance and dependence. In addition, opiates are hypnotic, mood altering, and affect mental clarity and physical response. Physical effects include constipation, reduced respiration, slowed heart rate, and perhaps pupil constriction. Morphine, an opium derivative, is typically injected under the skin. At greater than therapeutic analgesic doses, central nervous system (CNS) effects are heightened, eliciting a state of elation and euphoria. This effect is immediate after injection—a rush—a sudden orgasmic feeling in the abdomen, a warm flush. However, this orgasmic rush is not typical in people who snort or smoke opiates. The user's state of mind often dictates the intensity of the rush. If in an agitated, restless, depressed, or excited state, the rush is typically there. Side effects include nausea, and this nausea (for addicts) is addictive as it is the prelude to the euphoric state. Interestingly, morphine does not cloud thinking and does not affect physical coordination or slur speech—however, ability to concentrate is impaired.

First Aid: Overdose is a medical emergency; evacuate to medical facility where a medical professional may administer opioid antagonists with a high affinity for opioid receptors in the brain that block the effect, but do not activate them.

Note: Opiates are antidiarrheal, anti-dysentery, narcotic analgesics and have been used in medicine for thousands of years—the premier analgesic for pain and suffering. Humans have endogenous opioids that provide a gentle array of the same effects as plant- and chemical-based opiates. Hypothetically, near-death and death experiences provide a rush of endogenous opiates that may ease us euphorically into the next world. Morphine (named after Morpheus, the god of dreams) was isolated from opium in the 1803. The synthesis provided a more controllable and predictable drug for treating pain. Heroin, produced in 1874, was considered an improvement over morphine; it proved to have all the undesirable side effects of morphine but was faster acting. An analgesic dose of 5–10 mg causes (almost immediately) the following CNS effects: drowsiness, loss of inhibition, decrease sensory response, loss of anxiety, pain relief, pupil constriction, and slightly depressed respiration with impaired concentration. These effects usually lead to a dream-laden sleep.

PASSIONFLOWER

Passifloraceae (*Passiflora incarnata* and related species)

Identification: Up to 500 species of a perennial woody, climbing vine, with intricate, colorful, spoke-like flowers in blue, purple, red, and white.

Habitat: Native to the West Indies and southern America, worldwide distribution; partial shade, moist, well-drained soil across 7 climactic zones.

Toxins/Drug: Harmala alkaloids: harmine, harmaline, harmalol with sedative properties (known for many centuries) from the aerial parts of the plant (leaves, stems, flowers); used medicinally, ritually, and recreationally.

Symptoms: In small doses, passionflower produces a sedating, mild marijuana-like high. In high doses it is hypnotic—a mild hallucinogen. Also, at high doses, especially when mixed with other psychoactives such as skullcap, damiana, and cannabis, it has a monoamine oxidase inhibiting effect.

First Aid: Self-limiting. At high dose and in extreme cases, a serotonin antagonist may be administered. Emotional support is helpful to control excessive agitation (which may require a sedative).

Note: The plant's name coined by early conquistadores refers to the Christian crucifixion; others suggest it is related to the plant's aphrodisiac effect. Tea infusion had mild sedative properties. Fresh fruit eaten raw, juiced, or made into beverage with water, cornmeal, or flour. Fresh or dried leaves parboiled or panfried, eaten by Native Americans. In animal studies, infusion was sedative, antispasmodic, inhibited motility. Native Americans used infusion of crushed root for earache; also applied pounded root as a poultice on inflamed contusions, boils, cuts. German Commission E approved for treating nervousness and insomnia.

PEYOTE, MESCALINE
Cataceae (*Lophophora williamsii*)

Identification: Peyote is a desert plant of religious significance to Native Americans. It is a small cactus made up of buttons, which are the part of the plant consumed for the drug effect.

Habitat: Found in desert areas of Mexico, Baja, southwest Texas (Big Bend), Arizona. In Texas, north of the Rio Grande between Comstock and Big Bend, Native Americans who practice Native American medicine legally collect the cactus.

Toxins/Drugs: Alkaloid mescaline, N-methlymescaline, N-formylmescaline, N-acetylmescaline, and related alkaloids as well as hordenine, candicine, anhalamine, anhalanine, and other related chemicals. Mescaline belongs to a family of psychoactive drugs called phenethylamines. Structurally similar to amphetamines, phenethylamines have stimulating as well as hallucinogenic qualities.

Symptoms: Soon after ingestion, intense nausea and perhaps (but not always) vomiting. Hallucinations possible with increased sensory awareness to sound, feelings, and sight. It is a calming relaxant, leading to introspection.

First Aid: Symptoms may persist for 3 days. Observe and protect victim. Overdose may course the victim toward violence and depression (although rarely suicidal). Sweating increases as does heart rate and blood pressure.

Note: Combining mescaline with other drugs is dangerous. Originally, the mescal bean was used as a ritual/religious hallucinogen, but due to its potential toxicity the bean was replaced with the extract from the peyote cactus. Through an act of Congress, Native Americans have established the Native American Church that provides legal ritual use of peyote. By comparison with other hallucinogens, peyote mescaline requires a more significant dose to get the desired effect: A hallucinogenic effect from mescaline requires on average about 5 mg of mescaline per kg of body weight; a 150-pound person would require 325 mg of the drug—LSD is over 3,000 times more potent. The therapeutic use of this drug and other related hallucinogenic drugs including LSD for psychotherapy did not yield significant positive results in controlled studies with human beings. Studies suggest the plant extract is hypoglycemic, may improve endurance and courage, and may lessen hunger and thirst. Drug may not be addictive, but feelings of well-being may make the drug psychologically habit forming.

SAN PEDRO CACTUS
Cactaceae (*Echinopsis pachanoi* syn. *Trichocereus pachanoi*)

Identification: A fast-growing columnar cactus, stems light to dark green and occasionally bluish green, to 7" in diameter and up to 20' tall. Typically 6 ribs with spines in clusters of 5.

Habitat: High-altitude cactus (but not always) native to Ecuador, Argentina, Bolivia, Chile, and Peru; found in Mexico at lower altitudes and as an ornamental in California and Arizona.

Toxins/Drug: Mescaline used for healing and religious divination in the Andes mountains for over 3,000 years. The drug belongs to a family of psychoactives called phenethylamines. Structurally similar to amphetamines, phenethylamines have stimulating as well as hallucinogenic qualities. Plant constituents are N-methlymescaline, N-formylmescaline, N-acetylmescaline, and related alkaloids as well as hordenine, candicine, anhalamine, anhalanine, and other related chemicals. Amounts of the psychoactive substance vary from plant to plant, environment to environment.

Symptoms: Soon after ingestion, intense nausea and perhaps (but not always) vomiting. Hallucinations possible and increased sensory awareness to sound, feelings, and taste. Intense and rich colored visions reported with a calming, relaxing effect, leading to introspection and self-examination.

First Aid: Symptoms may persist for 3 days. Observe and protect victim. Overdose may course the victim toward violence and depression (although rarely suicidal). Sweating increases as does heart rate and blood pressure.

Note: I first saw this cactus in the Baja as an ornamental, and again in the Wirikuta Garden in San Jose del Cabo—a magnificent cactus garden with hundreds of varieties. San Pedro is cultivated in the garden in large numbers and is quite a sight to see. Then I stumbled across it at the community market in Ann Arbor, Michigan. This cactus may be grown for ornamental purposes in the United States but may not be processed for the psychoactive mescaline.

SALVIA DIVINORUM, DIVINER'S SAGE, SEER'S SAGE
Lamiaceae (*Salvia divinorum*)

SHUTTERSTOCK.COM

Identification: Species of sage in the mint family, having large green ovate and occasionally toothed leaves with yellow undertones. Leaves 4"–12" long, hairless, with little or no petiole. Plant grows to over 3' in height, with hollow, square stems that tend to break or trail on the ground. Flowers bloom (though rarely) in whorled clusters on a 12" stem, with 6 flowers to each whorl. Flowers are white, about 1" in length, curved and covered with hairs; violet calyx covered in hairs and glands.

Habitat: Salvia divinorum is endemic to the Mazatec region of the Sierra Madre del Sur mountains in Oaxaca, Mexico. It is found along streambeds and streamsides in rich soil. Plants sold and grown recreationally in the United States where legal.

Toxins/Drugs: Salvinorin A is the first documented diterpene hallucinogen, with low toxicity.

Symptoms: As explained to me by a user in Mexico: "It elicits a meditative state into spiritual realms of mysticism where I can explore the nature of consciousness and reality." This altered state of consciousness (consciousness expanding) is elicited by consuming the chemistry from the leaves. Mazatec people chew and swallow 10–20 leaves, and the desired effects come over a period of 10–20 minutes; the effects generally last for about 30 minutes, maybe up to 1.5 hours. Leaves are held in the mouth like a chew of tobacco, and the chemistry is absorbed through the oral mucosa; leaves can also be smoked or tinctured (alcohol). After the peak effects, normal awareness of self and the immediate surroundings returns. Short-term lingering effects differ from peak experience, and some users report an afterglow.

First Aid: Drug's action is self-limiting. Early research suggests that there is the possibility of long-term lingering effects. The drug is illegal in several states, and public opinion is forcing more legislation. Purveyors have said it is impossible to overdose with the drug. That may be hyperbole, but there is little information at this time on overdose.

> *Warning: Pregnant and nursing mothers should not use the drug, unless under medical supervision. Do not drive under the influence for at least 5 hours after initial consumption.*

Note: Salvinorin A inhibits intestinal motility, stemming diarrhea—this contraction-reducing property is most active on inflamed tissue, suggesting a use for chronic intestinal problems. It may also have an analgesic effect, possibly useful in drug-addiction treatment and polyneuropathy—research needed.

SWEET FLAG, CALAMUS
Araceae (*Acorus calamus*)

Sweet flag root

Identification: Long, flattened swordlike leaves, sweet, aromatic, primitive looking green, club-like flower. Plants found in large colonies in wet areas; temperate climate.

Habitat: Found in wet areas and edges of streams, primarily in eastern United States.

Toxins/Drugs: Volatile oils to include cis-isoasarone (American strains have less of this carcinogenic oil than foreign varieties), beta asarone, alpha- and gamma-asarone, and bitter principle acorone. Also tannins and sesquiterpenes: calamendiol, isocalamendiol.

Symptoms: Mild hallucinogen that is sedative and relaxant. Overdose may induce vomiting. The plant is antispasmodic, anticonvulsant, and a central nervous system depressant. A few herbalists chew or suck on the dried root (e.g., between the cheeks and gums) to keep them awake on long drives; however, it is not swallowed. Backpackers may find the herb enervating when they need it on a long hike. Like coca leaves, it tends to keep you going and delays hunger and thirst. One person says it lightens your feet when trekking. Effective sialagogue.

First Aid: Self-limiting. Long-term and copious use of high cis-isocarone and beta asarone *Acorus* may induce cancer.

Note: A subtle, thirst-quenching chew used to treat motion sickness and one of the most important plants of the eastern Native American tribes. Native Americans wore calamus leaf garlands as fragrant necklaces to mask body odor after hard rides and between baths. Peeled and dried root chewed as a sialagogue, stimulating secretion of saliva, quenching thirst. Root tea is an appetite stimulant. The aromatic, bitter root considered a stomach tonic to treat dyspepsia, gastritis. Triploid strains, having three times the typical number of chromosomes, are used in Europe and the United States to treat ulcers. The triploid strain produces about one-third the amount of the carcinogenic beta-asarone as Kalmus (Calamus) root oils from India; beta-asarone in ample amounts is carcinogenic to laboratory animals. Avoid long-term use and use only under the administration of skilled holistic health-care practitioner. Root traditionally used by pioneers (chewed or in decoction) to treat colds, coughs, fevers, children's colic, and congestion. I like to put the root in a pair of panty hose, throw it in a hot bath, and submerge my aching body for an aromatic, relaxing soak. In foreign countries, the dried root is ground and used as a spice and fragrance, but because of its beta-asarone content, these cosmetics are not sold commercially in the United States. Root fragrance may repel some insects and rodents.

TOBACCO, CIGARETTES, CIGARS, SNUFF, CHEW
Solanaceae (*Nicotiana tobaccum*)

Identification: Annual or biennial with many genetic varieties that grow to 10' in height. Stem is many branched with large ovate to lance-shaped leaves. Leaves are pointed and alternate; may be 2' in length—a large and impressive adult plant. Greenish-cream flowers are numerous in clusters, sepals to 0.5", with 2" funnel-shaped corollas containing 4 stamens.

Habitat: Originated in tropical and subtropical Americas and is widely cultivated in the United States, Canada, and various other places worldwide.

Toxins/Drugs: Alkaloid nicotine, tar, and volatile oils.

Symptoms: Nicotine is addictive, carcinogenic, euphoric, an appetite depressant, and both a stimulant and relaxant. Drug has laxative qualities, induces vertigo, and is emetic and worm expellant. It is anodyne, diuretic, and slightly analgesic (smoke of leaf). Internally the lethal dose of the pure drug is 40–100 mg. Ingestion leads to nausea, vertigo, and collapse. Nicotine is easily absorbed through skin and is toxic—potentially fatal.

First Aid: The best treatment is avoidance. Keep cigarettes and tobacco products away from small children. Do not ingest. Nicotine can pass through the skin upon contact with the juice. A small child ingesting tobacco is a potentially fatal medical emergency. A nicotine patch and/or nicotine gum used by smokers may help them kick the habit. Homeopathic cessation remedies are available, typically administered by professional holistic health-care providers. Acupuncture is also a successful cessation tool.

For every American who dies from tobacco use, more than 20 suffer from other serious tobacco-related illnesses. Individuals who had experienced major depressive disorder at some time in their lives are more likely to have a history of tobacco use than the population as a whole. Smokers with major depression were less successful at their attempts to quit than were either of the comparison groups. Gender differences in rates of smoking and of smoking cessation observed in the larger population were not evident among the depressed group. Research data indicates that when individuals with a history of depression stop smoking, depressive symptoms and, in some cases, serious major depression may ensue.

Note: Native Americans use the herb in rituals. As a sacred offering tobacco is considered a warrior plant and burned in sweat lodge ceremonies. Tobacco-leaf poultice is placed over snakebites, insect bites, and stings, and the juice is used as a potent insecticide. A pouch of tobacco is a considerate and appreciated gift when visiting Native American friends. Tobacco mixed with *kinnikinnick* (bear berry leaves) is smoked or chewed. Smoking tobacco raises homocysteine levels in the blood, making the smoker more susceptible to cancer, dementia, and Alzheimer's disease.

This is a striking garden plant, certain to amaze friends. Visit the Medicine Wheel monument off Highway 14A in the Little Bighorns of Wyoming and see Native Americans hang tobacco pouches and other gifts as offerings to the Creator. For more on medicinal uses of tobacco read FalconGuides' *Medicinal Plants of North America* by Jim Meuninck (Globe Pequot Press).

Bibliography

Jim Meuninck has several 2-hour DVDs that identify and demonstrate the use of edible and medicinal wild plants. For free and useful information, visit his website, herbvideos.com.

DVDs

Cooking with Edible Flowers and Culinary Herbs. Jim Meuninck and Sinclair Philip (60 minutes/DVD) www.herbvideos.com, 2013.

Diet for Natural Health. Jim Meuninck, Candace Corson, MD, and Nancy Behnke Strasser, RD (60 minutes/DVD). One diet for disease prevention and weight control. www.herbvideos.com, 1997.

Edible Wild Plants IV. Jim Meuninck and Dr. Jim Duke (2-hour DVD). More than 100 useful wild herbs documented, recipes demonstrated. www.herbvideos.com, 2013.

Herbal Odyssey. Jim Meuninck (CD-ROM). Interactive media with World Wide Web links covering over 500 herbs, edible plants, edible flowers, and medicinal plants. www.herbvideos.com , 2012.

Native American Medicine. Jim Meuninck, Patsy Clark, Estela Roman, and Theresa Barnes (2-hour DVD, 2005).

Natural Health with Medicine Herbs and Healing Foods. Jim Meuninck, Ed Smith, and James Balch (60 minutes/DVD), www.herbvideos.com,1997.

Survival X. Jim Meuninck. (2-hour/DVD). Self-reliance and survival skills demonstrated. www. herbvideos.com, 2012.

Books

AMA Handbook of Poisonous and Injurious Plants. Kenneth Lampe and Mary Ann McCann, American Medical Association, Chicago, IL, 1985.

American Indian Medicine. Virgil Vogel. Norman: University of Oklahoma Press, 1970.

Audubon Field Guide to North American Wild Flowers Eastern Region. New York: Alfred Knopf, Chanticleer Press Edition, 1992.

Audubon Field Guide to North American Wild Flowers Western Region. New York: Alfred Knopf, Chanticleer Press Edition, 1979.

Edible and Medicinal Plants of the West. Gregory Tilford. Missoula, MT: Mountain Press Publishing, 1997.

Edible Native Plants of the Rocky Mountains. Harold D. Harrington. Albuquerque: University of New Mexico Press, 1967.

Edible Wild Fruits and Nuts of Canada. Nancy Turner and Adam Szczawinski. Victoria, Canada: National Museum of Natural Sciences, 1979.

Edible Wild Plants. Oliver Medsger. New York: Macmillan, 1966.

Field Guide to Edible Wild Plants. Bradford Angier. Mechanicsburg, PA: Stackpole Books, 1974.

Field Guide to Medicinal Plants and Herbs of Eastern and Central North America. 2nd ed. Steven Foster and James Duke. New York: Houghton Mifflin, 2000.

Field Guide to North American Edible Wild Plants. Thomas Elias and Peter Dykeman. New York: Van Nostrand Reinhold, 1982.

Field Guide to North American Medicinal Plants. Jim Meuninck. Guilford, CT: FalconGuides, 2009.

Handbook of Edible Weeds. James A. Duke. Boca Raton, FL: CRC Press, 2001.

Handbook of Medicinal Herbs. James A. Duke. Boca Raton, FL: CRC Press, 2001.

Handbook of Northeastern Indian Medicinal Plants. James A. Duke. Lincoln, MA: Quarterman Publications, 1986.

Handbook of Nuts. James A. Duke. Boca Raton, FL: CRC Press, 2001.

An Instant Guide to Edible Plants. Pamela Forey and Cecilia Fitzsimons. New York: Gramercy Books, 2001.

It's the Berries. Liz Anton and Beth Dooley. North Adams, MA: Storey Publishing, 1988.

Medicinal and Other Uses of North American Plants. Charlotte Erichsen-Brown. Mineola, NY: Dover Publications, 1989.

Medicinal Plants of the Pacific West. Michael Moore. Santa Fe, NM: Red Crane Books, 1993.

Medicinal Wild Plants of the Prairie. Kelly Kindscher. Lawrence: University Press of Kansas, 1992.

Michigan Trees. Rev. and updated. Burton Barnes and Warren Wagner Jr. Ann Arbor: University of Michigan Press, 2004.

Native American Ethnobotany. Daniel Moerman. Portland, OR: Timber Press, 1998.

Plants of Coastal British Columbia. Jim Pojar and Andy MacKinnon. Edmonton, Canada: Lone Pine, 2004.

Principles of Neuropsychopharmacology. Robert Feldman et. al. Sunderland, MA: Sinauer Associates, Inc., 1997.

Sea Vegetables. Evelyn McConnaughey. Happy Camp, CA: Naturegraph Publishers, 1985.

Shellfish and Seaweed Harvests of Puget Sound. Daniel Cheney and Thomas Mumford Jr. Tacoma, WA: Puget Sound Books, 1986.

Sturtevant's Edible Plants of the World. U. P. Hedrick, ed. Mineola, NY: Dover Books, 1972.

Traditional Plant Foods of Canadian Indigenous People. Harriet Kuhnlein and Nancy Turner. New York: Macmillan, 1991.

Western Forests. Stephen Whitney. New York: Alfred A. Knopf, 1985.

Journals

Alexander H. Glassman et al., 1990, "Smoking, Smoking Cessation, and Major Depression," *Jounal of the American Medical Association 264*:1546–1549.

E. Widy-Tyszkiewica and R. Schminda, 1997. "Randomized Double Blind Study of Sedative Effects of Phytotherapeutic Containing Valerian, Hops, Balm and Motherwort versus Placebo," *Herba Polonica* 43(2): 154–159).

N. L. Benowitz, 1990, "Clinical Pharmacology of Caffeine," *Annual Review of Medicine* Volume 41: 227–228.

U. Engelmann et al., 2006, "Efficacy and Safety of a Combination of Sabal and Urtica Extrace in Lower Urinary Tract Symptoms," *Arzneimittel-Forschung [Drug Research]* 56(3): 222–229).

Seed and Plant Resources, Catalogs, and Information

American Botanical Council (512-926-4900; herbalgram.org). Ask for their book catalog.

Horizon Herbs (541-846-6704; horizonherbs.com). Rare wild plants, both edible and medicinal.

J. L. Hudson, Seedsman Catalog (jlhudsonseeds.net). Rare and unusual seeds.

Richter's Herb Catalogue (905-640-6677; richters.com). A free catalog of edible and medicinal plant seeds and live plants.

Seeds of Change (888-762-4240; seedsofchange.com). Free catalog.

Poisonous and Psychoactive Plants Websites

Air-purifying plants: webecoist.momtastic.com/2009/04/08/air-purifying-plants/

American Association of Poison Control Centers: aapcc.org

Entheogens website: erowid.org

Jim Meuninck's web page: herbvideos.com

Poisonous plants and pets (ASPCA): aspca.org/pet-care/animal-poison-control/toxic-and-non-toxic-plants/pet-care/animal-poison-control/toxic-and-non-toxic-plants

Poisonous plants list: aggie-horticulture.tamu.edu/earthkind/landscape/poisonous-plants-resources/common-poisonous-plants-and-plant-parts/

Psychoactive plant list: en.wikipedia.org/wiki/List_of_psychoactive_plants

Toxic houseplants website: lancaster.unl.edu/factsheets/031.htm

Index

Snuff, 83–84
Solanaceae, 4–5, 9–10, 45–46, 70–71, 83–84
Solanin, 4
Solanum, 13–14
Solanum americanum, 4–5
Solanum carolinense, 13–14
Solanum dulcamara, 4–5
Solanum nigrum, 4–5
Solasodine, 4
Solidago canadensis, 35–36
Sophora secundiflora, 74
Sophora tomentosa, 74
Soul vine, 64–65
Sowbread, 38–39
Spathiphyllum spp., 42
Split-leaf philodendron, 56–57
Spotted dumb cane, 50
Spurge, 19–20
Squirrel corn, 11
Star of Bethlehem, 56
Steroidal alkaloids, 47
Stinging nettle, 29–30
Strychnine, 76
Strychnos nux vomica, 76
Sweet flag, 82–83
Swiss cheese plant, 56–57
Symplocarpus foetidus, 18–19

Tanacetum vulgare, 30–31
Tannin, 18, 82
Tansy, 30–31
Tar, 83
Taxaceae, 60
Taxine alkaloid, 60
Taxol, 60
Taxus baccata, 60
Taxus brevifolia, 60
Texas mountain laurel, 74
Thebaine, 77

Thujone, 31
Tobacco, 83–84
Toxic cyanogenic glycoside hydragin, 53
Toxicodendron diversiloba, 28–29
Toxicodendron radicans, 28
Toxins, fruit trees, 59
Trichocereus pachanoi, 80–81
Triterpene saponins, 6
Triterpenoids, 22
Tropane alkaloids, 46, 49
Tulipa spp., 58
Tuliposides, 58
Tulips, 58

Umbelliferae, 13, 20, 24, 25, 26
Urticacea, 29–30, 31
Urtica dioica, 29–30
Urushiol, 28, 29

Veratrum viride, 12
Vetch, crown, 21–22
Viscaceae, 54–55
Viscum spp., 54–55
Volatile oils, 66, 83

Water hemlock, 20
Weed, 72–74
Western skunk cabbage, 21
Wild iris, 5
Wild plants, poisonous, 1–22
Wood nettle, 31

Yage, 64–65
Yaupon, 22, 51–52
Yew, 60

Zantadeschia aethiopica, 47
Zygophylaceae, 8–9

About the Author

Jim Meuninck is a biologist and counselor who, for more than thirty years, has studied the use of wild plants as food and medicine in North America, Europe, Central America, Japan, and China. He lives on the shores of Eagle Lake, in Edwardsburg, Michigan.